Shift Gears

MEMPHIS, TENNESSEE 38117

Shifting Gears

A cycling adventure across South America leads to mission service in England

GARY BISHOP

Published by:
New Hope
P.O. Box 12065
Birmingham, Alabama 35202-2065

Dewey Decimal Classification: B
Subject Headings: BISHOP, GARY
SPIRITUAL LIFE

Cover design by Barry Graham

Shifting Gears was originally published in part as *Six Wheels Northward*.

N924102•5M•0292
ISBN 1-56309-017-1

▲▼▲

Dedication

To my wife, Delores, and our two sons, Gary and Paul, whose love, faithfulness, and courage I treasure.

Acknowledgments

To all God's faithful servants who have helped us "along the pilgrim way." Many brought practical assistance; others challenged me onward for our Lord; all were God's instruments at important points. Without their faithfulness and keen perceptions, I would be the poorer. Some see from afar what the Lord is doing in our lives, others walk with us through valleys and victories toward our eternal home. It is our honor and privilege to have been in their company and to have shared their lives.

▲▼▲

Contents

▲▼▲

Foreword

I vividly remember the Sunday evening of October 2, 1977, when Gary Bishop was ordained into the gospel ministry by First Baptist Church, Havelock, North Carolina. Only God could have brought together such an improbable coincidence of people and circumstances—a young man from New Zealand being ordained as a Southern Baptist minister through a chain of events that included bicycles, high adventure on the highways and back roads of South America, a brush with death in the Atrato Swamp of Central America, and a life-changing prayer of desperation that eventually led to Gary's appointment (along with his wife, Delores) as a representative of the Foreign Mission Board of the Southern Baptist Convention.

In that ordination service, everything seemed to come together for Gary. He was there on his knees before God instead of riding high on an ego trip. His parents were there, having traveled all the way from New Zealand to support their son and see this transformation of their unregenerate prodigal into a new man in Christ—just as fiercely determined to reach his goals, but now heading in a new direction. George and Sue Downs were there—unique, caring, godly, missions-minded people who for a time served as Gary's foster parents in the faith in the Canal Zone of Panama. Gary's adopted church family, First Baptist Church, Havelock, was there, affirming his gifts through testimonials and encouraging the pursuit of his heavenly calling by their endorsement. And I was there, like a proud older brother, enjoying a

▲▼▲

special "holy ground" moment not just in Gary's life, but in the life of the highly esteemed and loved people whom I am still privileged to pastor.

One of my responses to Gary's ordination, however, was dead wrong. I thought that this traveling man's travels had come to an end, that he would now "settle down," that he had at long last, after many a mile, reached the destination God had set for him. As it turned out, Gary's stay with us in the Atlantic Association lasted only about eight years—including service with First Baptist as youth pastor, then as pastor at Cape Carteret Baptist Church and college student simultaneously.

With college degree in hand, Gary enrolled at Southeastern Baptist Theological Seminary, Wake Forest, N.C., where he graduated three years later. There followed a four year pastorate of the River Bend Baptist Church of New Bern, Atlantic Association, N.C., and from there appointment by the Foreign Mission Board as a Baptist representative to Leeds, England.

It may well be said of Gary, as it was said of John Wesley: "The world is his parish." Amazingly, the story told in *Shifting Gears*—as exciting and enjoyable to read as it is—is like a trip around the block compared to the subsequent travels the Bishops have made as foreign representatives. I suppose that is what I take away from reading *Shifting Gears*, namely, that no matter what we can imagine for our lives during our pre-conversion years, God's plans for us are always bigger than our own.

Dr. Don Hadley
Havelock, N.C.
July 31, 1991

▲▼▲

1

Swamp

In the midst of the Atrato

The blackness of the swamp night slowly and gracefully transfigured itself into a gray dawn. Shadows formed and began to move mysteriously across the stagnant water. Moist fern and tall lashes of green, knife-edged elephant grass pushed in on one side of our camp, while on the other side a cluster of black palm trees swayed mournfully in the light, early morning breeze. From the sharp edges of the palm fronds clung glistening droplets from last evening's rain; the droplets hung motionless, grew larger and fuller, and finally fell into the water below with an audible *plink*.

Another wet and soggy day in the great Atrato Swamp greeted us. In the confusion of waking and the returned awareness of physical discomfort, I slowly reoriented myself.

Ian, John, and I were struggling westward through the Atrato Swamp in northwestern Colombia, South America. We had cycled nearly 7,000 miles from Cape Horn to reach this uncomfortable, unhealthy environment which was now taking a devastating toll on our physical and mental capabilities. Dead and rotting foliage confused the eye. Everything was damp. The very air we breathed clung heavily to our lungs and seemed to stick deep down inside. The thick heat held our bodies captive and dictated our progress.

Now, as day dawned, the cries of nocturnal swamp creatures broke rhythm and ceased. Toads stopped their deep-throated croaks; fireflies dispersed, then finally disappeared. Quiet descended slowly.

The light grew and sounds of the day began. Flocks of migrant birds started to sing, interrupted by a few noisy parrots. Finally, in a nearby clump of spiked palms, the monkeys woke and commenced

▲▼▲

chattering and gossiping. They frolicked and ate, oblivious to our struggle for survival in the swamp.

In the brilliance of the yellow sun, the freshness of the new day began to unfold. Shadows shortened and retreated into the bases of the hollow trees and the depths of the fern roots. The foul water reflected the rays of the early sunlight that tiptoed across its smooth greasy surface. Foot holes that we had made when slinging our hammocks the previous evening appeared as black intrusions in the soft jungle floor.

In the distance echoed the cry of a howler monkey. I caught a quick, sharp movement as a gray speckled lizard skimmed across a nearby pool. He eyed the gently swaying hammocks momentarily, then with a flick disappeared into the reeds. More parrots flew overhead in threes and fours, squawking and piercing the morning stillness.

My eyes traced the hemp rope I'd strung from my hammock to the spiked palm that had sliced at my fingers the previous twilight. The droplets of moisture hanging on the rope grew slowly and then plunged into the water exactly as did those on the palms not twelve feet above us. The rays of light caught the droplets before they fell, flashing myriad colors as they changed position on the rope.

Their beauty, however, could not offset what hung beside them. My once bright yellow shirt and light fawn trousers were disintegrating from use and constant wetness. Seams had split and buttons were missing, legs were shredding, and pocket linings were useless. They smelled of stale sweat, putrid water, clinging fungus, and rotting fabric.

I peered through mucus-filled eyes into the new day. What lay ahead in this nineteenth day from the beginning of our swamp trail? I relaxed again to clear my blurred eyes. My left forearm tingled with discomfort as it brushed against the side of the fine mosquito netting. Continual slashing in elephant grass and sharp ferns had lacerated my hand and arm so badly that even the slightest pressure made me instinctively withdraw. My hand was scabbed, red, swollen, and ugly. I could still manage to slash effectively, but constant sharp stabs of pain were becoming increasingly harder to bear. I felt the tender flesh with my right hand and comforted myself, saying, "You'll be OK when you warm up," which was invariably the case.

A throb of soreness came from both my feet. I rubbed them together furiously in an effort to rid myself of the infernal itch. This

16

▲▼▲

was just another complaint created by constant immersion in water and lack of dry equipment. I moved slightly and was annoyed by the rash high in my crotch. "There's no cure for these things in a swamp," I told myself. Oil and sweat clung to my entire body, giving me a feeling of being encased in manure, from which I desperately wanted to escape.

A callused thumb rubbed against a three-day growth of whiskers on my thinning face. As I considered ridding myself of it, I heard the sounds of a sleeping bag zipper opening and a loud yawn from behind me. John had just greeted his day in the watery world in which we struggled to survive.As each of us tried to spur himself into action, we glanced at each other, and though we grinned childishly, we meant little by it. We both knew our thoughts were on the day's effort that lay ahead. Could we extract enough stamina to maintain our present rate of progress, slow as it was? Could we maintain our mental equilibrium? Could we muster the reserves for our continual fight against discomfort, infection, and insects? My mind always arrived at the same answer: "You've got to. The way out lies ahead."

John placed the assembled, half-pint kerosene stove on a misshapen tree root eighteen inches above water level and coaxed it to life. Its gentle, low roar meant that in twenty minutes our routine breakfast of oatmeal and milk would be ready.

Warm and dry, I slipped from my jungle hammock into wet, clinging socks, pulled my soaked leather boots on, and stepped into calf-deep water to reach for my shirt. The cold, nauseating slime stuck to my skin. These were the worst moments of the day as I transformed myself from a dry, warm-blooded New Zealand kiwi into a wet, bedraggled, unshaven, web-footed swamp trekker. Wading toward John, I tripped and almost fell into dead palm leaves. Awkwardly regaining my balance, I reached him and took over cooking. Ian was also up and proceeded to dress and organize his load.

The sun rose a little higher as the gray bubbling mixture that we called breakfast steamed in our aluminum pot. Any shadow that still existed took flight until late afternoon, which would see us a half mile nearer the Atrato River—we hoped!

"Can you mix the milk, John?" I asked, eyeing the oatmeal carefully.

"Be right there!" replied John, who was trying to roll up his hammock above the water and keep it as dry as possible.

▲▼▲

Ian beat John in rolling up his hammock and joined me to set out the three plates in the most level spots he could find.

"OK, John, it's ready," I said as I slopped it over the uneven plates. Nothing further was said until we had eaten all we could of the vile mixture.

I shot a quick glance from beneath my swollen eyelids at Ian, who was having difficulty even swallowing. John was unable to finish his helping. Standing on a tree stump, he scraped the remaining oatmeal into the foul water. Once the teapot had come to a boil, we wasted no time in sipping the sweet thirst-quencher.

It was time to move. The heat was becoming intense as the sun climbed in a sparsely clouded sky. Already we were sweating, and we hadn't accomplished so much as one more yard of distance. Ian helped me roll up my damp hammock while John crouched near the hot stove, packing food, cleaning plates, and gathering the necessary items for our midday meal. As usual, John and I would concentrate our day's efforts on hacking and slashing our track. Ian would move camp to the next small clump of trees and rig things up. This was so difficult that it would take him the entire day.

I was becoming concerned about our appearance. Signs indicating severe physical and mental exhaustion were unmistakably evident. Glassy, lifeless eyes stared blankly from swollen sockets, wet hair fell into our eyes, and our scalps itched continually. Cheeks were hollowed and sunken. Our young faces were bearded and untidy. Our shoulders and chests were lean, marked by many blemishes as a result of poor diet and uncleanliness. In saturated jungle boots my feet burned for relief.

"You ready, John?" I asked, impatient to get started.

"Yep, got everything. Where's the measuring cord?"

"Wouldn't have the foggiest idea!" was my ignorant reply as I began looking around for it.

After several minutes of slopping around our campsite, John discovered it already packed. We were doing things unthinkingly, often covering the same ground twice.

We said goodbye to Ian, told him to take it easy, and to have the teapot boiling at 4:30 when we returned. He wouldn't be taking it easy, though, we knew.

We left our old camp and companion behind. In water, fighting for balance in every stride, tripping over dead and cut vegetation, John and I moved out. The trail we had cut the day before had been reasonably on course. Only occasionally had we deviated due to small and sinewy hardwoods. High swamp growth pressed in on us as we stumbled along. Thousands of ants busily climbed water-soaked stems, looking for nourishment and intruders—us! These minute creatures added to our discomfort. They clung to us, biting furiously. In a matter of seconds they had penetrated into the remote corners of our bodies, making it impossible to continue until we had cleaned them off.

Finally we reached the spot where we had finished the previous day's cutting. There in the tangle of reeds and spindly growth lay three bicycles awkwardly out of place in a swamp. The track, just wide enough for one man and his bike, ended a few feet ahead. Swatting away big green-eyed horseflies, we stared at each other.

"Right, let's get with it. Who's cutting first?"

"You are, laddy," smirked John.

"I am?" was my dry response. "OK, you win. Pass the file."

After sharpening my machete, I glanced up at John, who was looking in our lunch bag for the compass, and noticed his broad smile. He was probably very happy I'd taken first shift. With compass in my right hand and machete in my left, I turned to face yesterday's freshly cut trail, and pushed my weight backward into the dead branches, crackling fern, and thick green grass at the trail's end. The foliage bent slowly under my weight, exposing its coarse stems and supporting me for a second or two. I slashed quickly to sever them, and then, to keep my balance, took a long stride backward. In doing so I exposed more uncut stems and roots for my thrashing eighteen-inch machete. The ants resented the disturbance of their otherwise peaceful habitat and took full vengeance on my aching, sweating body.

"Little sods!" I exclaimed as I slapped the back of my neck with a swollen left hand. "Get off!" Stopping only made their biting seem worse, so I pressed onward.

At uneven intervals John showed up with one bike or another as he ferried them along the crude narrow track I had hacked. His broad frame barely squeezed by, and often his heavier weight dragged him deep into an oozing hole. He brought one bicycle after another over the ever-deepening rut until he sank almost to his knees.

For approximately an hour we toiled at our respective tasks and

▲▼▲

then changed for the next hour. The sun had climbed high and burned our saturated shirts. As the breeze died, the stuffiness and humidity became overpowering. At the switch I removed my shirt, cut a hole in the root systems by my feet, watched the water settle, and drank my fill. Even this filthy refresher was welcome.

Having quenched my thirst, I plunged my ant-riddled shirt into the same hole, drowning several hundred ants. Satisfying myself that all were dead, I wrung the shirt out and bathed my chest, neck, and shoulders. Only after this was I ready to continue with my newly allotted job. Although we longed to talk a little at the changeover, we held our task paramount, so we limited our conversation to a few short sentences.

John's bulk pushed heavily against the greenish-topped growth as he swung his razor-sharp machete deep into the network of stalks and stems. I watched him momentarily, then waded back along our sinking track for the last bike.

My way was obstructed primarily by John's large foot holes, which were impossible to avoid. As I stumbled along, without warning I tripped and slid into a hidden hole to the right of the path. In a split second I had sunk to my waist in putrid water. I could feel no bottom as both my legs were trapped. In vain I tried to move them, but the ooze I had fallen into held me firm from the waist down.

I groped for anything stable that would act as an anchor. Everything around me seemed too small, too soft, or too dead. Then, several feet in front of me I spotted a rotting tree branch protruding practically onto the track. Yes, that would do, but could I reach far enough? After one try I realized my arm was too short. If I wanted out of this mess, I'd have to lie down full length in the mud and water to grasp it.

Water washed over my chest and face as I gritted my teeth and strained every joint and muscle to reach the branch. My fingertips touched the decaying bark. For a moment I lay fully extended like an elastic band held at both ends, and breathed in lungfuls of distasteful air as I recovered.

Yet, was this effort in vain? Would the branch be too decayed and snap at the slightest weight? My grip tightened as I started very carefully to pull myself out. The branch groaned. For a moment I froze, eyes wide and unbelieving! It held, however, so I continued to tear

20

myself slowly, agonizingly, from suction's grip. Again and again the branch groaned in protest, but it continued to hold long enough for me to finally kick my feet free. I rested, covered from head to toe in mud and grass. My mud-spattered face smiled in satisfaction as I sighed and climbed to my feet. What a place to exist, I thought, as I proceeded once more along the trail.

Stumbling through the mud was second nature to us, but wheeling the bikes was an art we had to learn. We had removed pedals, chains, and sprockets in an effort to streamline them. If we were smart enough we could lean with the bike and therefore transfer some of our weight on it. On my return trip I went wide to the left in order to miss the hole that had claimed me before, and found John still cutting. We switched jobs twice again before stopping for lunch. Pre-cooked, cold, sweetened rice and two cups of tea would half fill our stomachs until dinner time.

"Lunch, John-o," I called, unpacking the front bag.

"Be right there, laddy!" he replied as he cut a hole to get a drink.

He knelt beside the hole, watching the impurities settle. Soon he would be able to drink without filling his mouth with weeds and minute parasites. Although we hated our watery environs, we also realized their importance for our own survival. We knelt in water as we ate our meager portions, hoping that someday we would once again enjoy red beef and freshly baked bread.

"What's your estimate on distance, John-o?" I queried through a mouthful of rice.

"How the blazes would I know!" came his sharp reply.

Trying to overlook his comment, I raised my voice a little and said, "Just thought you might wanna guess at it, buddy. That's all."

It was obvious from our conversation that swamp life was having an adverse effect on us both.

We changed the topic to the better times we'd enjoyed in Lima and Santiago and what we were likely to do when we finished our mammoth ride.

Our aching arms and backs yearned for longer relief as lunch time ended.

"Time to go," snapped John, unsheathing his machete. "Chuck the file, laddy."

He caught it above his head in two fingers and openly praised himself for his magnificent catch. We could have quite easily lost it and been in trouble since chances of finding it again would have been slim, and the spare file was back with Ian. Carefully John drew the file the length of the blade. Small metal filings dropped into the pool of water between his legs. The steel rang as he put the final touches to the razor edge.

I packed the lunch fixings into the small black bag and snapped it firmly to my front rack. This done, we spent the afternoon the same as the morning, fighting the wilderness for every yard of ground gained.

As the sun sank rapidly into a reddening sky, I pulled the final bike up beside John.

"Call it a day, John-o, it's time to head back to Ian," I urged, glancing at my watch.

"OK, I've had about enough anyway." He heaved deeply, wiped his perspiring face, and looked for a place to cut a hole for water.

After slinging the black bag over my shoulder, I grasped one end of our twenty-meter tape so that we could measure the day's toil. John would walk to the end of the nylon cord, mark his spot, and carry on.

"Just in time for tea," Ian chirped as we neared the new campsite he had spent all day organizing.

"Whadaya mean? If it hadn't been ready, sport, you would've been as popular as a dehydrated toad."

"Here, grab this," Ian said as he handed me a steaming cup.

"How in the blistering blue blazes do you expect a joker to drink it at this temperature? Give a guy a break, will you?"

I couldn't resist the dig and carried on, noticing John's red face as he took his first hot mouthful. He rudely spat it into a nearby, slimy, stagnant pool.

"Hey, got any purified cold water here, Ian?" John queried as he aired his throbbing mouth.

"Only one canteen and that's it," Ian answered.

"OK, chuck it over, please."

John took several hurried gulps and relaxed as it cooled his mouth and throat.

"Don't take it all, Johnny Boy," I said. Grinning, he passed it over.

The smoke climbed lazily into the failing light as we sat on damp moss-encrusted stumps and devoured our supper of rice and, this time, a little dehydrated meat and vegetables. Any variety was wel-

22

come, for it was badly needed. I looked across at John. His face was wringing wet from sweat and water. Small blemishes dotted his serious face and two days' beard covered his chin. The lifelessness of his eyes was emphasized by the exhausted pallor of his complexion. We were both used up, although John was the stronger.

Choking on the last mouthful of dry rice, I tossed my spoon into the aluminum plate. Then, wiping my mouth with a mud-smeared hand, I got to my feet and began to wade through calf-deep water.

Mucus clung persistently to my eyelids and blurred my vision. My legs had ached for relief for several hours and now my feet were dragging. After washing my utensils, I awkwardly made my way toward the hammock and a well-earned eleven-hour rest.

Off came my wet clothes. My body was glad to be rid of their irritation. Rashes and rub marks had appeared inside my thighs and arms. The skin was inflamed, raw, and sensitive to every movement.

The last things to come off were my wet, rotting jungle boots. The suction that held them to my feet was incredible. After I had freed myself, I hung them upside down on a branch for the night.

The mosquitoes, wasting no time in finding a warm-blooded body standing knee deep in swamp water, attacked immediately. Days of this had made me an expert at sliding into my hammock as quickly as possible. Unzipping the net, I shot in. Then began our nightly game of hide-and-seek. After the final mosquito had been obliterated, I began to examine my body for parasites. I searched carefully and was satisfied with finding only two large brown worms hooked into my calf. The sores on my legs were tender as I gently dabbed at them with a damp towel.

With heavy hands I cradled and wiped my face, thankful that I was again safe inside my hammock. My towel doubled as a pillow. The day's happenings ran through my mind. I could see the deep hole where I had stretched to my limit, only just managing to pull myself clear. I felt the soreness of the lacerations on my left hand and forearm, and remembered the tall elephant grass. Again the thought came to me, as I knew it did to my two companions: How many more days would we have to repeat these experiences? I turned slightly, easing the discomfort of burning thighs, only to feel the stirring, unsettling sickness of intestinal parasites.

Thoughts of my health and our monotonous diet lingered until

▲▼▲

memories of my mother's cooking replaced them. How wonderful it would have been just to have the pleasure of her company tonight.

Feelings of deep love for my family filled my heart suddenly. I recalled situations that had occurred years ago: how my mother had loved to prepare my favorite dishes when I visited home; how they were all so interested in what I was doing! The way Dad would ask how the farm life was going. If it was spring, he'd say, "Many twins this year, Gary?" And I'd answer yes or no and go on to a different aspect of the farming process. We might sit for an hour exchanging ideas and views while enjoying the comforts of our home. Their concern and loving interest that I had taken for granted I now held dear.

These events and, in fact, everything except swamp life, seemed to be gone forever, especially the people to whom I had said good-bye two years before in New Zealand.

▲▼▲

2

Discontented

Growing up in New Zealand

The dust of the sheepyards blew skyward as thousands of heavily wooled ewes trotted through the main holding pens. Their familiar smell was pleasing to my nostrils. I tethered my sweating bay gelding to the fence, feeling proud and sad at the same time. We had just brought in the largest mob of sheep for their annual shear, 2,500 in all. Dogs barked noisily, forcing stragglers into tightly packed pens. Now the yards were crowded with panting, bleating sheep.

Machinery roared in the shearing shed. I climbed the shed steps for the final time, immediately becoming part of the hustle of activity. Heavily muscled shearers expertly robbed each ewe of four to five pounds of wool in just a few minutes. Shed hands threw each fleece across the wool table, exposing badly soiled sections. These were discarded. Then they rolled the good fleece and stacked it to await pressing. No sooner was one finished than, with a flurry, another fleece was flung across the table. Wool covered the floor. I took one last look at the shearers, hesitated, then walked slowly away.

My horse stood patiently while I unhitched it. I led it up to the homestead of my aunt and uncle, carefully slid the saddle from its broad back, patted its flank, took off the bridle, and said a quiet good-bye. In the distance I could still hear the hum of the shearing shed.

Lifting the smelly saddle to its peg, I thought how wonderful it would be one day to spend all my time on this farm. Why were school vacations so short? How could anyone understand how sad I felt when I had to return to the city and school? How could anyone even begin to understand my love for animals and the wide open spaces of New Zealand? It was inbred, deep, vital, and ever-present, part of who I

25

▲▼▲

was. I could not get away from it. It was in my very blood.

My train left Rotorua for Auckland the next morning. We arrived at the station to hear the belching locomotive's whistle, preparing to depart. I shook hands with my aunt and uncle, climbed aboard, and settled in for the five-hour trip home.

By midafternoon we were chugging through the outer suburbs of Papatoetoe, my hometown. Houses replaced green farmland and children played where animals had once grazed. The train slowed and stopped at the station. There was Dad; he'd probably been waiting for a long while. I was glad to see him and tell him all that had happened in the last three weeks. He knew I loved farm life and that I'd likely wind up working the land.

With a welcoming grin he greeted me on the platform. "Well, Son, how was the holiday?" he asked.

"Pretty good," I replied, not knowing where to begin.

"How are Uncle and Aunty?"

"Oh, they're OK. They're shearing now. The last day I was there, we brought in the biggest mob of sheep and I was riding and then we lost some—and I like horses!"

I bubbled with excitement over farm life. I couldn't have cared less how anybody else was or what the weather had been like.

On the way home I continued to fill Dad's patient ear. He smiled as he listened, knowing what I meant since he had been raised on a small farm. Arriving home, I was greeted warmly by Mum and my brother Douglas.

"Where's Lynne?" I asked of my younger sister. "Away playing?"

"She should be back soon," Mum said, putting the final items on the dinner table. When she arrived, we ate dinner, talked more about my holiday, and then finally retired for the night.

The beginning of school was disorganized, as usual. I was starting the 12th grade. Students gathered and exchanged vacation experiences while waiting for the teacher to get started with lessons. Latin wasn't exactly a subject I excelled in. I didn't need Latin to raise crops or build stockyards. It seemed to me I didn't really need it at all.

After high school, I looked forward to a profitable future in a rewarding career. The rolling pastureland, typical of New Zealand, stretched in all directions. The blanket of greenness sprang from rich volcanic soil and would support five or six ewes per acre. Pines and firs dotted the landscape, adding their own beauty to an already refreshing scene. Sheep and cattle were always on the move by shepherd, drover, or giant trailer. A person might run into mobs of several thousand anywhere along the highways. The land, exceptionally rich, produced meat, wool, and a variety of citrus and vegetable crops. This was the life that beckoned me, and the call to it was irresistible.

My family took me to my uncle's farm, situated ten miles southeast of the North Island city of Rotorua. The spacious white homestead overlooked the lake and the island of Mokoia. We drove past the painted front gate that bore the name *Burnhill*, then up the steep concrete drive to the homestead. Two days later they left to return to Auckland. As I watched the car descend the drive, I choked back tears, realizing for the first time that I was 150 miles from home.

With the awkward enthusiasm of a seventeen-year old, I learned to drive heavy farm tractors and agile landrovers. The station (farm) had to be highly mechanized to retain peak productivity. Organization and careful timing were necessary to run over 6,500 ewes and 500 head of cattle. My uncle, who had spent a lifetime on the land, expertly controlled pasture rotation on his 2,000 acres. I greatly admired his judgment and skill, and learned a lot from him.

I spent a great deal of time reading. Everything from parasitic control in animals to brush chopping, from cropping to winter management and fencing fascinated me. I was far more interested in this than in listening to my Latin professor. Instead of the odor of a musty classroom, I now experienced the wind, rain, and sun of slowly changing seasons.

Spring had always been my favorite time of year. Pastures freshened and grew in response to warmer temperatures. Stock grazed contentedly. Ewes welcomed new offspring, caring for them as well as they knew how. At dusk young lambs left their mothers to play and frolic with each other near a clay bank or stream. Yes, this was the time I enjoyed the most, this time of new life; I enjoyed seeing things grow and flourish.

In the spring of my first year I was given my very own pup, which would grow up and eventually work sheep. Uncle Ron brought him over from Gisborne in a cardboard box. "He's yours, Gary. Take good care of him." With tender hands I reached in and stroked the little bundle of black and tan fluff. What would I name him? His frightened brown eyes gazed back into mine when I lifted him up onto my shoulder. He was mine. I was responsible for him. Even then I loved him dearly and looked forward to watching him grow. What kind of dog would he be? Would he be a yard dog, a huntaway, or an eye dog?

If he were to grow into a good yard dog, he'd have to have a loud, deep bark. He would have to be able to work sheep all day for weeks on end. For that he'd need a deep chest and strong, well-muscled forequarters.

To become a well-trained huntaway he'd need the ability to cast out in any direction I cared to send him, go around the sheep, and then return after pushing a mob from one side. He'd also need a good loud bark and be able to use it as he ran out, headed, and then returned. Physically he'd be almost identical to a yard dog. Actually, some dogs are equally efficient in both roles. The important thing is to keep them trim and not allow them to become overconditioned. Handling big mobs of sheep with a heavy, slow dog in steep hill country is not an enviable situation.

I liked to visualize my dog as an eye dog, one that would slide quietly and swiftly alongside a lambing ewe and flick her to the ground. He would be silent, his dark penetrating eyes concentrating on the sheep in question. A good eye dog must be a quick, lightly built dog of average size. His thinking capacity exceeds that of the ordinary huntaway or yard dog; with a movement or a fake, some eye dogs can shepherd. He must learn to use his mouth, not to tear or rip flesh, but to hold tightly and firmly to the sheep's muzzle to keep her from struggling. Owning a pup and having all these exciting discoveries to make thrilled me.

I would have to wait almost a year to find out about Tan, the name I gave him. I was convinced I had a trial champion just waiting to win an award at an annual sheep dog show. In the meantime, I had to train him. This started as soon as I'd won his affection and trust.

Observing the way he barked and moved in close quarters while still a small pup, I found that Tan preferred the open paddock. One Sunday I unchained him to take him out for a trial run, mustering a small mob of separated ewes. I kept him behind until we stood just inside the paddock gate, and then watched out of the corner of my eye for his reaction. His gleaming eyes were attracted to the woolly creatures; his black and tan ears pricked to pick up the slightest sound.

We stood together. I said nothing as I watched his black body tremble with excitement. Still I remained quiet, wanting to see just what his next reaction would be. I moved my boot forward half a pace and he came right up with me, near my leg, still shaking as he watched the sheep in the distance. His small head turned quickly in my direction, then just as quickly focused back on the sheep. I reached down to pat his head and, to my surprise, his concentration didn't waver.

Finally, the anticipation and excitement got the best of him and with a yap-yap growl, he lit out toward the grazing sheep. As far as he was concerned, any sheep would do as long as he could chase it. His little legs pounded the grass, but a small seven-month-old dog is no match for grown livestock.

He ran his heart out for about five minutes, then as I walked toward him, he returned to me, tail wagging and tongue hanging, as if to say, "Well, I tried, but they're just a little too big for me." I crouched in front of him and smiled as I patted his heaving chest. It was good to have the answer to my question: he definitely had the huntaway instincts. With correct handling and care, Tan could become a good mustering dog; he might eventually even double in the yards.

Time passed and my pup became a young dog, showing promise, full of his own importance and ideas, but only half-trained. I took him with me one day when we were felling bush in the high country. As we left for home that evening, he was not to be found. I whistled my lungs out, but I couldn't see Tan anywhere. With a heavy heart I returned to the homestead, wondering where he was. He never returned to his kennel. After a week of hunting, I accepted the fact that he was gone.

Shortly afterward I bought two other trainable dogs, since without canine companions my shepherding ability was nonexistent. Who ever heard of a sheep farmer without dogs? I had good luck with these two. They both responded to my training and learned quickly. With one more dog I would have a complete team, sufficient for my work. The final dog was black and white, a very strong eye dog, sensible and fast, and extremely capable for lambing, when silence is golden. His name was Moss and he was my special pride.

My ability to complete various tasks increased. At the end of my four years, I could do most of what was required of me. I was able to muster large mobs of sheep alone, drive tractors with heavy implements over bad terrain, kill and dress mutton, shear sheep, ride horses, chop bush, and erect miles of fencing. As my farming experience widened, so too did my participation in sports. My spare time was consumed with table tennis, boxing, squash, and surfing, but I still was able to spend time on dates and parties. My life was stimulating and intensely satisfying.

Now, at twenty, I sought security. I envisioned a small holding of 400 or 500 acres. With this much-desired financial security, I would be able to marry if I wanted and raise and support a family. To stand squarely on my own two feet without the assistance of others was my aim. To have comforts up to my own standards and to share them with my young family was security. I wished to own a nice house with well-kept gardens and lawns. I wanted a car and sufficient credit to travel and do as I pleased. These were the things that interested me. They would rust, decay, and fall apart, but they were what my selfish, materialistic mind wanted. A young man needed money and plenty of it, not only to replace antiquated possessions but to enjoy the prime years of his life.

However, as I scrutinized the economic situation, I became increasingly aware of ever-darkening horizons. No young man, no matter how keen and knowledgeable, could fight this one-sided battle and come out ahead. Farming was heading into a serious recession that only men already established would be able to survive. I saw many young farmers crumble under the heavy burden of bad prices, mediocre seasons, and tight money. The outlook was not good. So I turned my back on the life that I loved and gave my attention to more lucrative situations.

I said farewell to my uncle and aunt and joined my family again, but in a new location. They now owned a fresh fish business, and I accepted their offer of employment. The shop was on the eastern coast of New Zealand at the small mining town of Waihi. My folks lived six miles away at Waihi Beach. The white sand and tumbling surf stretched for five long miles. In the summer months the crowds gathered, business boomed, and everybody was on vacation. Christmastime is during the New Zealand summer and the spirit of Christmas abounded; people were richly tanned and overly endowed with holiday dollars.

Life inside was strange after being almost exclusively outdoors for years. We toiled side by side over boiling hot fat, potatoes, and fish. Dad's business sense was good, and we had a high profit margin and successful living. But I yearned for the open spaces, the smell of dry hay, and the tempo of the shearing shed. I missed the feel of my dog's damp nose and the motion of a galloping horse.

After the holiday makers had retreated from the sun back into the cities, I left home for the second time, seeking better money and a more attractive life. As I sped toward Napier in Hawkes Bay, I was unaware of events that would change my immediate plans.

Napier was an average-sized city, set in the heart of the citrus and fruit-growing area. From this region came some of the highest grades of wool and stud-breeding stock. Farms were grazed intensively. The land was rich and fertile, selling for high prices. The climate was fresh and warm with the good rainfall necessary for fruit and crops.

Amid the activity of the advancing shearing season, I searched for a position in a wool-scouring plant. After only a few days' search a manager phoned me with a job that started that very night.

The company ran on a twenty-four-hour basis, and my shifts alternated every week. Our hours were long and tiring, but the paychecks more than compensated for that. When I was able I joined a table tennis club and once again looked for a suitable boxing gym. My life was full and active. I was standing squarely on my own two feet and earning good money, living life the way I wanted. I thought life was a battle in which only the fittest survived. The weak sank into despair and self-pity. Who cared about them? I certainly didn't.

But then questions began to come to mind. What was left after a whiskey-soaked Saturday evening except a Sunday morning when I tried hard to hold my head together and stop the thunder? What was left after a hard day's work and a few beers under my belt? What was the point of a car, money, and a young healthy life? What was everybody looking for? Were they really happy?

I loved my family dearly and often wondered what would happen when they died. Deep in my heart I knew that God was an existence, a force, a power, and figured that when I died I would naturally go to heaven. Didn't everyone?

When I was ten, my sister and I had attended a Baptist Sunday school every week for a couple of years. I took part in various classes and even passed a quarterly exam with honors. Along with other boys my age, I learned and prayed with my teacher, but I was never told God's plan of salvation. Looking back, I realize the classes were more academic than spiritual. Our interest waned and we slid back into the usual lazy Sunday of the secular world. Church no longer had a place in my life. With varied interests, and a headful of pride and masculinity, life was too full for religious services. I always had more important things to do.

None of my friends felt the slightest commitment and, like me, were bent on material pleasure. We were all basically empty. It was expected that we would cut a man down behind his back, curse and rant with rage at complaints or when circumstances didn't please, and feel harassed and frustrated because things were not going our way.

For several months I worked at the wool-scouring plant. Then I met Ian Hibell and something drastic happened. Ian would help to change my life.

▲▼▲

3

Breaking Loose

Preparing for the journey

I had just finished supper in the company dining room. My watch showed 2:47 A.M. Saturday morning. I was bleary-eyed and smelled of grease and sweat. Sitting across from me was the Englishman on our shift, trying to eat an egg sandwich while sleeping. I grinned and coughed loudly. His left eye twitched and the right one showed no sign of opening. I coughed a second time. This time two eyes half opened while his jaw kept moving rythmically.

"Mmmm-ah! Must have dozed off," came his reply. He stretched, groaned, and climbed off his stool.

"Time to relieve the others," I said, stepping toward the battered screen door.

We moved out to our respective jobs, both of us exhausted. Saturday morning was always the worst shift as it was the last one of the week, and by then everybody had had enough. I stopped, turned, and watched Ian walk to his job.

"So that's the guy who was crazy enough to cycle here from England. I'll bet he's been to some pretty interesting places. Sure would like to know him better," I said to myself. I dragged myself away from my dreamy thoughts and went on to my job.

During the next few weeks opportunities presented themselves for Ian and I to share experiences, and I learned a lot about his bicycle tours of America, Canada, and the Far East. He related the stories with relish and enthusiasm; I sat wondering at the things he had seen. To my surprise he was only staying in New Zealand long enough to save sufficient money for another cycling tour—this time from the south-ernmost tip of South America to the northern tip of Alaska. I could not

▲▼▲

understand why anyone would wish to have such a way of life. Then I began to see that touring was to Ian what farming was to me. When I came to that realization, his enthusiasm was easy to understand.

When he spoke of Indonesia, his eyes sparkled as he vividly described his experiences. Sometimes I was breathless, sometimes I was speechless, but most times I was green with envy. Ian fueled my imagination. Then one day he hit me with the question: "Why don't you come with me to South America?"

"What?" I exclaimed, stunned by his question.

"You don't have a thing to lose, Gary," he insisted.

That's true, I thought. Besides, I was thinking of taking off to Australia when the season ended.

"You're young, fit, and strong. Why don't you think about it? I'll bet you'd never live to regret it."

I thought, I've never ridden a bike seriously in my life. Oh, forget it; if he wants to go, let him. I'll go to Australia instead.

"Well, I'll think about it," I said, for want of a better answer. With that I changed the subject and filed everything away in the back of my mind.

It was a dream, never likely to become reality. More pressing details of life needed my attention and careful organization. For instance, how was I to spend this next weekend? I was celebrating my twenty-first birthday—an important occasion in New Zealand—in two months, and I hadn't even decided whether I wanted to turn twenty-one. My parents were asking me where I wished to celebrate: in Napier or at home. Not knowing the answers to these simple questions, I couldn't possibly contemplate an issue that might change my life!

Ian finally persuaded me to move to the Clive Youth Hostel where he lived, and in the ensuing months I met many young foreign travelers who stopped there for a couple of nights. John Bakewell was a fellow New Zealander staying there, a big man my age and from a similar farming background. We had a lot in common but, strangely enough, we didn't get to know each other quickly.

I first saw John at the hostel on a wintry night. Ian and I had just finished eating a good steak meal and were relaxing before the fire. John walked into the circle of chairs, shook hands with several of us, and introduced himself. It was soon obvious that Ian and John had already met and that Ian had filled John's ears, too, with persuasive

▲▼▲

talk about bicycling to Alaska. They talked about the trip in a vague manner; the departure date was still over a year away.

This was the first of many discussions. Over cups of tea they gauged what funds would be required and whether or not each could save enough. My mind took in all that was said, and I reconsidered joining them. Which would I rather do: go to Australia and work on oil rigs and farms, or take two and a half years off to see South, Central, and North America? The cycling trip could yield greater financial return. Coupled with this was the probability of nationwide recognition and the success that accompanies such an endeavor. What did I want: a quiet flight to Australia, or fanfare and publicity?

On the plus side, I was confident of my own physical fitness, and I reckoned I could manage to push a ten-speed bike 20,000 miles from Cape Horn to Alaska. But I knew that if I accepted Ian's offer, my life and opinions would undergo drastic change; furthermore, we would arrive in Alaska absolutely broke and in need of work. If I were to spend my savings on an overland trip of this nature and magnitude, something beneficial had to come of it, because I was not prepared to part with over $1,500 just to see some foreign countries. Ian, however, had had experience working in Alaska and assured me repeatedly that I could make big money on the North Slope at whatever I wanted to do.

I entered their conversations periodically, but for the most part was only an interested listener. I was surprised when I found out John had definitely made up his mind and was looking for a better-paying job to raise money for the trip. In a short while, he moved over to the western provinces of the North Island to work for a steel construction firm. With John 250 miles away, Ian and I settled into our ordinary work routine.

The cycling trip gradually became a challenge; I found myself wanting to see if I could do it. My success in many sports made me feel I was more than able. I was sure of my strength and ability, proud of how and what I had learned. And so about one month before my twenty-first birthday, I decided I'd take the gamble and stake everything on reaching Alaska.

If we succeeded we would be the first team to make the trip completely overland. Our trek would commence at road's end, Tierra del Fuego, Argentina, and would terminate at road's end north of Circle

▲▼▲

City, Alaska. Our purpose was to complete the 20,000-mile ride under our own power. Riding in a vehicle when we could either cycle or walk with our bicycles was strictly forbidden; boarding a passing vehicle when things became tough was out of the question. The only river transportation we would allow ourselves would be the bank-to-bank direct crossing of a deep river. If the trail did not resume on the other side, we would cut through jungle and reeds until we reached it. This was to be a serious attempt to go from the bottom of the world to the top, completely and unequivocally overland. We realized from the outset that we faced hard times and knew our purpose would be severely challenged in the Atrato Swamp of Colombia and the Darien Jungle of Panama.

I considered these aspects as well as I could before making my decision. Only one detail remained: I wanted to make sure my family agreed to what I wished to do. My love for them was deep and strong. Although I was turning twenty-one, legally able to choose my own destiny, I would leave them grieved if they opposed my going. My birthday celebration would be something of a bombshell, since I planned to tell them that evening.

I had delayed the celebration until a suitably long weekend so that the invitations would have a better than average chance of an affirmative answer, and on the appointed night our house was brimming with people and noise. It was good to see relatives who had come, some a long way, to celebrate my final acclamation of independence. I had been living on my own for a couple of years, but tonight's celebration made it official. Speculation about the response of family and friends to my pending announcement kept popping into my mind as I greeted people and opened my gifts.

The air soon became heavy, filled with laughter, cigarette smoke, and guitar strumming. Conversations sprang up in various corners of the three occupied rooms. I noticed Ian was sharing stories with a group of my young cousins, who sat fascinated, enthralled, and some even infatuated. Only Ian knew how my feelings were churning deep inside, for I had told him that if my family was against this trip, I would reconsider.

My mother and others had prepared a buffet big enough to satisfy the appetites of the entire beach population. There was something to eat for every taste and whim. My birthday cake sat decorated and glit-

▲▼▲

tering, waiting to be cut, the central point of the table.

Thoughts of delivering a birthday speech made me cringe. I did not care for formalities. Still, everybody expected the birthday boy to say something, I thought to myself. Clearing his throat to get everyone's attention, my dad welcomed our guests and said a few words about me that made me feel important, privileged, honored, and proud.

Then everyone's attention was focused on me, and I immediately turned bright red, hung my head, and said as little as possible, rather badly. Twenty-one years old, but I still couldn't pluck up sufficient courage to tell them I wanted to see South America. Cameras flashed as Dad, Mom, and I cut the cake. I had blown my speech clear out the windows; now as we prepared to eat and later sing, I felt frustrated beyond words.

I weaved my way into Lynne's conversation and finally threw out the hook. My own frankness shocked me. I swallowed a half-chewed lump of turkey, took a sip of beer, and repeated the idea with elaborations. She listened silently. My beautiful, well-meaning, intelligent sister looked at me with radiant green eyes and agreed with everything I said. She understood perfectly and even thought it was a good idea, "if that's what you want."

Naturally our conversation was overheard, and the word soon traveled throughout the house. Everyone was smiling and agreeing with one another that I had a wonderful opportunity to see the world. Many shook my hand, patted me on the shoulder, and wished me well.

Mom's reaction was reserved, but I could read her face clearly. She cared only for my happiness; if going overseas was what I wanted, she was happy for me. Yet I could tell that she didn't want to see her second son leave. There was joy, but also sorrow, as she anticipated waving farewell to me from the wharf. She'd not be part of the things I liked and said and felt when we left in nine months. The different dishes and puddings that she delighted to please me with couldn't please a son not there to enjoy them.

Dad was 100 percent behind our venture, for he knew the value of expanding one's horizons through travel and different experiences. He had served during World War II in the Middle East, Italy, and North Africa. His support was solid and very meaningful to me, since I

▲▼▲

respected and loved my father more than any other man on earth.

It appeared that my going overseas was a fairly popular decision and, at last, my mind was free of any concern. I had the backing of my family, foremost, and of my friends, support that was to strengthen my personal dedication and purpose in the tedious eighteen months that lay ahead.

Around noon two days later, Ian and I left the beach to drive back to Napier. As dusk descended and we neared the rich mud flats of Napier, a crimson sun disappeared behind the cultivated green farmland. Driving parallel to the Pacific Ocean, we sped toward the Clive Hostel. The breaking surf thundered against the pebbled bottom as darkness crept across the water. My birthday weekend had been wonderful. Now, the months ahead would be cluttered with work and preparations for the trip; I'd have very little spare time.

The hostel would be our base camp. Here, in Central Hawkes Bay, the first completely overland expedition from Cape Horn to Alaska would be birthed.

We were three men with an idea, a spirit of adventure, and a will to succeed and tell the world. The sense of a challenge to meet and overcome spurred us on, as did the rewards we could not yet visualize but were sure lay beyond it.

Were we strong enough to challenge the Andean Mountains? Our route lay directly through them. What lay ahead in the unknown and sparsely populated jungles of Panama? We found information to help answer such questions in the city library. Seated around a heavy oak table, we studied books and maps, fascinated by the length and vastness of the South American continent. We carefully noted geographical differences as we picked alternate routes. Patagonia, a vast area in Southern Argentina and Chile, was unavoidable. This dry, windblown region stretched nearly 1,500 miles northward from the Cape. Crossing the Andean belt would be the next test; then we assumed we'd have easier going until we plowed into the great Atacama Desert north of Santiago, Chile. We pondered our route repeatedly.

Next, we focused our attention on the Darién Gap, a 300-mile stretch of tropical jungle separating Colombia and Panama. Charts showed a yearly rainfall of approximately 130 inches, one of the highest in the world. The map showed only a projected road through this almost impenetrable rain forest. Once past this section, the rest would

▲▼▲

be easy. But to achieve our goal of making the entire trip from Tierra del Fuego to Circle City under our own power with our bicycles, we would need to walk into Panama via this back entrance and link up with roads as soon as possible.

Ian looked up and smiled. "It looks as though we're going to have quite a walk."

"Yeah, looks a bit that way, sport," I replied dryly. "Let's worry more about that when we're nearer, shall we? Like maybe next year?"

"OK," came his answer as he returned the battered atlas to its shelf. "Blimey, we're late for our appointment with Tom. Come on, we'd better get going!"

We scrambled down three flights of stairs, jumped in the car, and sped down the streets toward Hastings, ten miles from Napier, to make our selection of bicycle tires and innertubes. Tom, the cycling shop owner, had made special orders for us and given our expedition priority since we had a deadline to meet.

He greeted us with the usual, "Hi, boys. How's things been? Reckon you'll make your time limit?"

"At our present rate of progress, Tom, no," came Ian's reply.

We chose equipment and placed the order in Tom's capable hands. We left with a smile and a good-bye, bound now for the canvas merchant who was making front bags to our specifications. This man was extremely busy and slightly unreliable, but an expert at his job.

I left Ian waiting in the car and ran into his untidy, noise-filled workshop. Shaking his hand, I hastily inquired as to what had become of our front bag order.

"Haven't had the slightest chance to do 'em," he said from behind his chattering machine.

"Could we have them by the end of the week? We need 'em." I spoke loudly over the roll of brown canvas.

"See what I can come up with. Call back Thursday."

"Right! You're on," I said. Stepping across yards of tangled string, I left him intently sewing.

A quick glance at my watch showed that the time was twelve noon. We had one hour before we were due to start our shift. I slid behind the steering wheel, started the car, and headed for the small township of Clive, halfway between Napier and Hastings.

"Next stop Clive Post Office," I said.

▲▼▲

"Yep," answered Ian. "I wonder whether our cycle builder in England has completed your frame yet?"

"If he hasn't by this late date, he'll be really popular!" I answered.

"If he hasn't sent them by now, it'll mean they'll have to be sent airfreight, and that'll cost you and John a packet, Gary," Ian responded.

It was a sobering thought, because to send frames and wheels airfreight plus the expense of packing would cost us approximately $200 above our planned expenditure.

I waited impatiently in line at the postmaster's counter. Finally my turn arrived. He greeted me, then shoved half a dozen items of mail into my eager, waiting hands.

"Thanks. Must get going. We're late for work. See you tomorrow." I turned on my heel, threw the mail to Ian through the open window, and slid in the driver's seat.

"Not a thing from England," said Ian as he thumbed through the mail.

"What does the guy think he's playing at?" I queried, frustration mounting. "Here we are six short weeks from departure and no bikes to ride. Great!"

Ian and I silently smoldered at this turn of events. All our plans had come unstuck. Pannier bags were late and needed alterations. Chains and sprockets didn't arrive in time; in desperation, duplicate orders were sent to Australia. Fortunately, we were able to purchase two sets of Campagnolo cranks and chain rings in time, the only ones the dealer had remaining in stock. We shelled out more money on international telegrams to our frame builder in England asking him to complete immediately the custom-ordered bicycle frames and send them airfreight at the earliest possible opportunity; then we waited anxiously for word that they had arrived.

At this stage, just one month before we were to leave for South America, most of our secondary equipment had arrived. To our delight, one afternoon when we returned from work, there on the front lawn sat a six-by-six-foot packing case fresh from England. Our frames had finally arrived. With hammer and screwdriver I tore into the box eager to hold my special frame that would carry me to Alaska. I carefully unwrapped it, making sure I didn't so much as breathe unevenly on it. There it was, made to my measurements, our design and my

40

gold color scheme. John's was there also, bright and new, a bigger frame for a bigger man; his chosen colors were gray and mauve.

That evening Ian and I worked late into the night assembling bottom brackets and chain wheels, and positioning hubs and axles. It was good to see before my own eyes $500 worth of machine slowly take shape. Our dream was almost a reality after months of frustration.

We planned our gear in detail. Ian would carry in his front bag, strapped to handlebars, a repair kit, his camera, overflow of bulk food, some dehydrated food packages, shaving kit, personal papers, money, and letters. In his rear panniers (a pair of bags that hung over the rear wheel) would be bulk food bags holding three or four pounds of rice, oatmeal, sugar, powdered milk, flour, and some raw vegetables. He would also carry matches, spare parts for the kerosene primus stoves, and other items. In his japara bag, strapped on top of the rack, he would carry a sleeping bag, a lightweight mountain tent, his clothing, tent poles, and a fly sheet.

In John's front bag would be personal papers, camera, film, a small medical kit, gloves, bread, and sometimes fruit. The rear panniers would hold a frying pan; three aluminum plates; three knives, spoons, and forks; three cups; his diaries; clothes; and some food. In his japara bag he would carry his sleeping bag, three space blankets, a windbreaker, jacket, and dehydrated food.

My bicycle's front bag would hold two half-pint kerosene Primus stoves, camera, lighting fluid, and gloves. The rear panniers would carry dehydrated food, my clothes, diaries, tea containers, bulk tea, bulk vegetables, jacket, and my windbreaker when not in use. In my japara bag I would carry my sleeping bag plus smaller plastic nonspill containers of sugar, milk, tea, vegetables, and fruit when available. In the very backs of our panniers both John and I had ordered special pockets, each made to carry two quarts of kerosene for the primus stoves.

The circled date on the calendar drew nearer as Ian and I brought the final tasks to a close. John was bringing things to a close in New Plymouth and was brimming with anticipation.

A few weeks before leaving I sold my car and rode my new bike as often as possible, making minor adjustments with it running smoothly along the tarred surface. The thin tires whined as they skimmed the hot asphalt. My legs enjoyed the powerful circular motion as the chain meshed silently from sprocket to sprocket. In my mind I was already in South America.

With our final paychecks in our pockets, we said good-bye to the firm we had worked with for two years. They extended their best wishes to us, and our friends said farewell. The local newspapers had heard of our proposed trip and requested a story and pictures. The articles appeared, basically erroneous.

The day for our departure grew nearer. Ian and I packed only the amount of gear required for our 20,000-mile ride and said good-bye to the Clive Hostel and Hawkes Bay.

We met John in Palmerston North; he had ridden south from New Plymouth. We spent one night there, exchanging ideas and talking over small things to be done once we hit Wellington.

The following day, with ninety miles to ride to reach Wellington and our boat, we had breakfast and left at 8:30 A.M. The main highway was well made and in excellent condition. We were pleased with our fitness and realized that our previous months of training hadn't been in vain.

We were to stay at the home of my relatives, and we arrived just as dusk was descending. Rain clouds hugged the bush-clad hills that pressed into the capital city. Awaiting us were Mum, Dad, and Lynne, who had journeyed down by car to say farewell. In the midst of this meeting, we completed last minute frenzied preparations.

Near the last night I talked with Dad about different things. I valued his comments and his concern and faith in me. Neither of us knew what lay ahead, but underlying everything he said was a quiet confidence that I couldn't fully comprehend. He had had experience with overseas countries; he had insight into the awkward and dangerous situations and hardships I might experience. He accepted my desire to see for myself other cultures and, above all, to see if I had the capacity to keep going when things turned bad. Most importantly, Dad understood why a man had to do what he felt he must.

My father was a quiet, moral man with a good sense of humor. During my early teens he had taken an active interest in my activities and was pleased to see me do well. I appreciated his interest tremendously, and later my only regret was that we never studied the Bible or prayed together. Occasionally we would say grace before a meal, but family discussions about Christ just never occurred. The plan of salva-

▲▼▲

tion was never clearly defined. My only spiritual instruction was what I had received in the year or two in the ineffectual Sunday school of my childhood.

My mother, like any mother whose children decide on a venture as crazy as what we planned, was concerned. I spent time going over our route with her and trying as best I knew how to reassure her that nothing would happen to me. With tears in her eyes, she agreed with what I said, but I could see that Mum was literally counting the remaining time that I would be with them. Our last meal, our last actions, our last words all held a special meaning for her, as they certainly did for me.

Finally, one evening, the last hours for time together were over as we said good night. The next morning we would leave on a 6,500-mile boat trip to Cape Horn.

Throngs of people crowded the wharf, waving and cheering farewells. Streamers were tossed back and forth as the familiar song, "Now Is the Hour," echoed through the already vibrating air. After dismantling our bikes and stowing them as unobtrusively as possible in our cabin, we found our way up on deck to see my folks and hundreds other well-wishers. My heart skipped a beat as I hugged my mother good-bye and shook my father's strong hand. I was happy, but I was leaving my homeland and my loved ones for at least five years. Now as I viewed them in the colorful crowd, I noticed that my mother was crying as she waved. My sister also was badly shaken as the full impact of my leaving made itself felt. My own eyes burned as I waved back. I noticed my dad standing, deep in thought, possibly reliving his own departure from New Zealand years before to go to war.

With a purposeful shudder the great engines stirred the green-blue waters and shortly we were heading into the channel for the open sea and Cape Horn. When I could no longer see my family, I slowly descended to our cabin, knowing only too well the uncertainty that lay ahead.

▲▼▲

4

Six Wheels Northward

From Tierra del Fuego through Patagonian Argentina and across the Andes to Santiago, Chile

The alarm clock rang noisily. It was 4:30 A.M., December 7, 1970, and our last morning aboard the liner, *Achille Lauro*. Our trip east from New Zealand across the Pacific was about to end. We dressed in our warmest clothes and ascended to the first deck to view the bleak beauty of the Strait of Magellan near the southernmost tip of South America. The cold wind penetrated our jackets and pants as we stood awed by the towering mountains and glaciers.

Mist clung to the jagged, desolate peaks, a grim reminder of what a New Zealand mountaineering team would encounter. This team of five, with whom we had become acquainted during the voyage, had come to climb several peaks on the island of Tierra del Fuego. I thought to myself, *I'd rather ride my bike than risk my neck trying to climb some treacherous glacier.*

Along with the rest of the passengers keen enough to get up at this hour, we wildly snapped shots of the rugged scenery. The dark gray water, chilled by antarctic currents, swirled dangerously through the narrow channels. We kept to the center of the channel for the most part, slowly churning a wake of troubled water. Glaciers slid steeply into the straits on either side, sheer and uninviting. The grayness of the mountainsides and bare rock was in direct contrast to the fertile green of New Zealand, now half a world behind us. The extremely low temperature and biting wind soon made it impossible for me to manipulate the camera effectively. We were chilled to the bone, so we returned to the heated interior for an early breakfast.

During a leisurely breakfast of bacon and eggs, the 25,000-ton liner slowed, then finally anchored in the Strait of Magellan. Punta

▲▼▲

Arenas lay on the gentle rolling hills that sloped toward the sea. From the deck, this southernmost city of Chile seemed stark and lifeless, with a gray summer sky as a backdrop.

Passengers were anxious to get on dry land again, so at the earliest opportunity most boarded the Chilean landing vessel, *Melinka*, to be transported to their first South American landfall. We were content to stay aboard, however, until most of the tourists had left. We lunched aboard ship with our friends from the New Zealand climbing expedition, said our farewells, and then went to pick up our bicycles. Through narrow corridors we pushed our sparkling bikes, slipped down the gangway, and finally reached the safety of the landing boat.

In fifteen minutes, we drew alongside the battered timbers of the Punta Arenas wharf. Cargo boats were strung out on either side, handling steel and timber from the northern ports of Chile. Almost as soon as we had set our gear on the wharf, we were surrounded by an excited crowd of bystanders. I noticed their coarse features and brown skin, the clothes they wore and, of course, the way they spoke. To the south, beyond the glistening hull of the *Achille Lauro* we could see the low flat island of Tierra del Fuego.

Our intent in this mammoth cycling endeavor was to ride from the southernmost accessible trail on the South American continent to the northern extremity of trail at Circle City, Alaska. Punta Arenas was not the beginning of our trip, for still further south, on the tip of Tierra del Fuego, was the port city of Ushuaia, and beyond this, by rutted track, La Apatia. (There were several smaller islands still further south, but they were tree covered, mountainous, and inaccessible.) La Apatia would be the beginning of our northward thrust. In order to ride north, we would have to begin by cycling south.

We soon cleared Chilean customs and entered Punta Arenas. After three days in which we prepared our gear, purchased food, and adjusted as best we could to a new climate and surroundings, we rode down to the same wharf where we had arrived after our ocean voyage. We boarded the same ferry that had brought us ashore then, but this time it took us south, thirteen miles across the channel to the island of Tierra del Fuego, the Island of Fire. The western side of this island is owned by Chile and the eastern side by Argentina. It is the main island of the Tierra del Fuego archipelago. Cold antarctic spray and biting winds are nearly all I remember of the two-and-a-half-hour voyage.

▲▼▲

Water pounded the little *Melinka* as she struggled forward through swirling currents.

As our craft navigated Porvenir Harbor, the quietness here was in direct contrast to the waters we had just crossed. There, nestled among the windblown hills of Tierra del Fuego, rested the major town of Porvenir. Slowly the *Melinka* picked her way up the channel to the beach where we'd land. With a surge of diesel-driven engines, she charged the sandy beach and held firm as the captain lowered the front. We were able to leave only after a truckload of sheep and bulls had disembarked. Ancient trucks were in regular use in this part of the world, a sight strange to our eyes. Once on the island roads, we were able to do the first real riding of the tour. Not used to the weight of the laden bicycles, nor to the roughness and softness of the road, our journey to the hotel was slow and cautious.

The houses along the road were made from lumber or corrugated iron. Each had a rusted and blackened chimney, since heat was impossible without their coal stoves. Electric power was generated, but it was available only during the hours of darkness. Most cooking was done on ranges, and this alone normally kept the insides reasonably cozy.

Cold and hungry, we stepped inside a homey-looking hotel. The smell of food greeted us, and the warm air hit our reddened faces. We strode into the tattered dining room, sat down on old, chipped chairs, and glanced around. The proprietress greeted us. We ordered our meal, then inquired what she would charge for a room. It was inexpensive, so after eating we carried our bicycles upstairs to spend the night. That night the wind howled outside, finding every crack and crevice of our cold room, but under thick, warm bedding we slept soundly.

The new day dawned clear, cold, and blustering. After breakfast we said good-bye to Porvenir and started our 300-mile ride which would take us east to the Argentine border and then south to the end of the road on Tierra del Fuego. Heavy gravel hampered our speed and stability for most of the morning, but once we became accustomed to the road surface and ferocity of the wind, our time improved.

The sharp, irregular chips and rocks on the road tore tread from our new tires. In a short time they were scuffed and severely weakened in numerous places. We carried spares, but at this stage we would not change them unless it became impossible to ride safely.

Gary takes a break to shave in Patagonian, Argentina. Gary, Ian, and John arrived in Ushuaia, the southernmost city in the world, in December 1970—the starting point of their challenging journey.

▲▼▲

The fifty-or-sixty-mile-per-hour wind occasionally helped us along the winding road, but more often buffeted us, so spills were frequent. Our road took us past large estancias (land estates or cattle ranches), and occasionally we took shelter alongside one of their barns to prepare a meal. Through wind-filled days, bucketfuls of grit and dust blew into our already smarting eyes. All the clothes we possessed were now covered with dust, and our ruffled hair harbored countless grains of the stuff. I had brought only minimal clothing: one wool jersey, one pair of long trousers, three short-sleeved shirts, two pairs of cycling shorts, two pairs of socks, three changes of underwear, one windbreaker, and a pair of gloves.

Pools of sparkling water near the roadside provided the only washing water. We halted near one to wash. Gently we laid our bikes alongside the road and for one short moment stood mirrored in the clear water.

"Who's first?" I asked.

"After you!" Ian shouted above the wind as he focused his camera for an early-expedition shot.

With a shiver and a deep breath, John dipped his hands in, bent low, and brought about a cupful of icy water to his crusty face.

"Fine. One more before you're through, John," enthused Ian as he reloaded his camera.

John called for his towel and, after handing it to him, I gave my face, neck, and arms the identical treatment.

Chilly water soaked deep into the pores, almost stinging. The refreshing jolt on the back of my neck was followed by a handful of water in my eyes. Any remaining sleepiness was forgotten. Ian followed after packing his camera; then together we continued south to the small town of Ushuaia, Argentina.

This stark scenery, with its continuous winds and decaying animal life, continued until the 4,000-foot pass which stood in the range of mountains between us and Ushuaia. As we rode up into this range, we came first to some light growth, then trees, and finally wooded areas that crept persistently up the mountainsides. Springs trickled from unseen crevices and dripped from sheer rock faces. The small valleys were now green instead of tussock brown, with soft grass instead of bristly spikes of brush and fern. This then gave way to rock face and shale as we climbed above timberline.

▲▼▲

The climb to the summit of the pass was the steepest and straightest of the tour. Halfway up and in our lowest gear, we had to quit. Ahead we could see the top, but with a full supply of food and an approximate one-in-eight gradient, it proved to be a pass we couldn't conquer on wheels. It was the only one in South America that brought us to our cycling knees.

Snow clung to the highest gulleys and depressions as we descended back into greenness and away from slick shale and sheer, uninviting rock. Back in timber country, the road meandered into town. Argentine workers muffled in heavy jackets and caps watched bewildered as we jolted our way into the central plaza and main commerce center of Ushuaia to buy more food and, most of all, honey.

Having bought the required supplies and packed them into our small bulk-food bags, we now asked the bystanders about the end of the road. With final instructions fixed in our minds, we pushed out from the small Argentine port against the usual sixty-mile-an-hour side wind. Gravel and dust blew past us. It seemed as if nature were trying to erase our marks from the gravel roadway.

Braced against this wind and pedaling steadily, we found the tract that took off from the road. It continued, and so did we, riding over rocks, cattle prints, wagon ruts, and through mud-bottomed pools until finally we broke out on an expanse of green farmland: La Apatia. There stretching before us lay the chilled waters of the horn.

A squatter's timbered hut stood 150 yards from the shore, his bay mare tethered not far away. In the right foreground stood cattle pens that probably had been sawed and shaped from the very timber that had once covered his small holding. The backdrop for this lonely, beautiful scene was a forest-covered national park that continued down to the three small islands that actually form the famous Cabo de Hornos (Cape Horn).

We surveyed the scene in quiet thought. This was really the end; there was no more trail. Today we had finally reached the starting point of our 20,000-mile ride. Close to one another, we bent and touched the ocean we would never see again and never really wished to.

We shook off the drops of water and extended our hands to one another. With a broad grin, I looked Ian square in the eyes and said, "It's worth it—all our frustrations and setbacks—just to be here with a fantastic experience ahead. Next time we shake hands it's on the Arctic Circle, Alaska."

"You bet," came Ian's happy reply as we turned to remount and find a spot to camp in that windy, lonely place.

It had been a quick six days to reach La Apatia from Punta Arenas, since we had the assistance of a tail wind for most of the distance. It was December 16 as we wove our way back north to Punta Arenas. On this return trip, the prevailing west wind slowed our pace alarmingly. All our physical stamina was required to reach Porvenir by Christmas Eve.

Anxious to be in Punta Arenas by Christmas, we wasted no time boarding our friendly ferry, the *Melinka,* that gently chugged across to the Punta Arenas Harbor.

Back into the familiar city we rode, full of confidence and happy that it was Christmas. Ian, a seasoned traveler, had been away from England for eight years. John and I had spent all our yuletide seasons with our folks in New Zealand so this one would be unusual. It was hard for me to think of anything else but home. I remembered only too clearly the fellowship and love shown by my family to all who chose to call. Our home was, more than ever, open to all at this time of year. The Christmas spirit flowed through and from us and it was wonderful to belong.

This Christmas we prepared our own dinner in a hotel room. Over two Primus stoves we cooked our meat, dehydrated food, and the precious New Zealand steamed pudding we had carried from Wellington.

With a full stomach and glassy eyes, I relaxed on my uneven, sagging bed. Thoughts of what they were doing back at Waihi drifted through my mind and I knew they were wondering just where I was and wishing, too, that circumstances could allow us to be together for the holiday season. Christmas for me had always been a time of sun, surf, and sand. It was a special season when I let the mundane things of life slide and enjoyed to the fullest the weeks of freedom. Spiritual significance to the holiday was zero. Although we exchanged gifts, I was totally oblivious to the one gift God had sent for me personally. Here in Punta Arenas I had only an overwhelming loneliness for my family.

Two days later, on December 27, we left the small Chilean town

▲▼▲

behind and headed due north on our selected road, Ruta 40.

The terrain seemed to be against both progress and mental stability. We pedaled our hearts out for days in an effort to gain a toehold on South America, battered day and night by gale-force winds that raced from west to east, stubbornly making a slow twenty-two miles each day in our lowest gears. The land was desolate, devoid of greenery, and punctuated only by an occasional pinnacle. Ragged and tattered fencelines stretched to infinity, to be swallowed by tussock and sand. Prolonged winters made it a frozen wasteland for many months. The population was one person per square mile. Estancias spotted the countryside; the people eked out a living while fighting snow, ice, or wind every day of their lives.

Next we entered the vast Argentine portion of Patagonia, a place as flat as a table but covered in spiny, brown tussock. The badly potholed road was sunken and heavily eroded by heavy transport and lack of maintenance. Sharp rocks and gravel nicked and gouged at our Michelin tread, tearing precious layers of cording and further weakening the tires.

We were buffeted from the left by intense winds, so that riding on the wrong side of the highway was the only possible way to remain on top of the cycle. This gave us the entire width of the road to straighten and continue forward when we were blown off course. As we grew tired, spills from our bikes became more frequent. After a fall like this, I'd regain my feet (leaning into the wind), pick up my bike, dust it off, examine it, and ride on. This happened many times each day. At any time a wheel could have buckled and been bent beyond repair. In that case a bus ride to the next town big enough to carry bicycle accessories would have been necessary. That would be one big hassle! Each of us hoped fervently that it wouldn't happen and that we could make Santiago, Chile, our first exchange base.

This was not to be. Shortly after leaving Rio Gallegos, and just after passing one of the now-familiar estancia houses, I was struck from behind by a pickup that slid ninety-six feet before hitting me.

With the wind howling about my ears, I was unable to hear the warning yell from John who always rode behind me. When realization of danger dawned, I desperately tried to pick my way through piles of loose gravel to give the vehicle room to pass, but I was pinned to the central track by two furrows of gravel and the wind. The pickup suddenly seemed very near. The hair on my neck stood erect as I knew I was about to be hit by a truck! When it came, my feet were free (there was no pull at my ankle or knee joints); I was out and flying through the air. I landed with a sickening thud and tried in vain to regain my feet. No luck. Everything seemed to stop. I felt pain in my left leg, and my left hand was bleeding.

These events happened in a split second; then all I felt was pain. My bike looked like a mangled piece of 531 tubing wrapped around the front axle of a Ford pickup. Venom dripped from the voices of John and Ian as they scolded the uneasy Argentinian for his thoughtless driving and excessive speed. Strong arms gathered me up and placed me inside the truck. The driver drove us back to the Estancia Hotel Aike which we had passed not twenty minutes before, and arrangements were made for a room for one mighty sore cyclist.

On careful examination, we found that the rear wheel of my bike was damaged beyond repair. A new rim, tire, and tube would have to be purchased in Rio Gallegos. Our ability to communicate in Spanish was woefully inadequate, but John had the best grasp of the language and was the one who would have to make the trip and grapple with the frustrations of misunderstanding. He might not have an extensive vocabulary, but he had the brashness of ignorance and the persistence to try until he was understood. Both Ian and I always fumbled awkwardly over the smallest idiom and expected our lamentable pronunciation to be immediately understood. John caught the one and only bus for Rio Gallegos in hopes of getting back in three days. By then we hoped the bruises and lacerations to my leg would have passed the worst and be improving.

During our forced stay at the estancia, we had an opportunity to observe Argentine gauchos in their natural environs. For a large part of the year they were snowed in; in this season, their summer, the wind blew continuously and froze the earlobes right off the side of your head. They all drank the traditional *mate*, a tealike beverage made from the leaves of a species of holly, for comfort. Clothing was heavy and ragged. Large dark-colored scarves were wrapped around their brown necks, and on their heads they wore battered, dirty berets or some other kind of hat. They seemed weather-tired and lacked enthusiasm for anything.

As I lay on my bed I wondered what made Montiel, the estancia

▲▼▲

gardener who became our friend, stay there. Born in a small town farther north, he had come south to earn the higher wages available on
the oil rigs that drew up crude oil. He had worked on a rig for two
years until an accident broke his leg and retired him from that rugged
life. Now Montiel held a secure position on the estancia, maintaining
the extensive garden that provided a large variety of vegetables for
their own consumption. He seemed much more alert than his fellow
workers and was always clean and better dressed.

The oldest gaucho, with a tired, lined face and a growth of beard
that should have been removed five days sooner, took charge of my
treatment. Studying the blackness of my left hip, he grinned as he
pressed the area lightly with his coarse fingers and said a few sharp
sentences to a bystander. In a little while the medication arrived, and
without further ado he rubbed the ointment into the bruised area. For
three days he returned to repeat the treatment. His only gestures were
a smile and a wave since he could not understand us; our Spanish was
too inadequate to converse with him. At the end of the third day he
motioned for me to try to stand. With his aid I took my first few
painful steps.

One more day and we would leave. John had returned on time
and my bike, with a new twenty-six-inch wheel, was ridable again.
Our departure hinged only on whether I was ready. I wondered
whether my hip would take the pressure of a prolonged hill climb or
hour upon hour of leg motion, but I knew both John and Ian were getting impatient. I'd find out soon enough if my leg would perform.

When we had packed our bikes and readied ourselves, we shook
Montiel's hand and left him with tears in his eyes. A good-bye cheer
was delivered to the old gaucho who had doctored my bruises and
whose name I never knew.

Once back on the road we faced the same icy blast for another
three weeks as we rode north through Argentina until we crossed
through the Andes into Chile again via the Bariloche Pass. Patagonia
had taken its toll in equipment, expense, and strength. We were now
all tired and planned to rest when we got to Osorno before riding the
248 miles to Santiago, the throbbing capital of Chile.

The western side of the Andean mountain chain was green and
fertile, far removed from arid, coarse, brown Patagonia. In southern
Chile, grapes, tomatoes, vegetables, and all varieties of fruit grew. We

▲▼▲

encountered towns frequently on the concrete Pan American Highway as we pushed to an unexpected fifty miles each day. Our cycling environment had changed dramatically. We were now on the first paved road of our South American tour.

When we reached the small city of Osorno, we bought supplies necessary for a two-day halt. On the city's outskirts lay cultivated green pastures with pigs and cattle and fields growing corn and assorted fruit crops. It was here that the Rio Rahue, a medium-sized river, ran cool and bubbly from its source in the Andean foothills to the Pacific coast.

Scuffling down the dusty rock-strewn road's edge, we found a green area large enough to pitch our mountain tent. Amid the wind-caressed willows, green lupines, and tall grass, we made our long-needed halt. The sound of flowing water fell strangely on our ears. Shoes were discarded to refresh our feet in the crystal stream fed by snow from the heights from which we had just come.

It was a pleasure to stretch my body on soft, lush, uncut grass and enjoy the coolness of the welcome shade. The breeze had now changed from a westerly to a southerly, and I knew it would push us forward to Santiago. My eyes searched the willows above to catch sight of the birds that darted in and around the soft branches. The sun in the clear blue sky welcomed us, a reward for our previous struggles. I glanced at my watch; it was 3:40 P.M., Saturday, March 6.

I studied the scene before me, so beautifully painted by the Creator of all the heaven and earth. A river ran nearby, lined with round white stones and squat willows. The tall poplars in the background were only just showing signs of autumn. The tall grasses swayed in response to the south wind. Our light blue tent moved and caught the sun's last rays, anchor lines alternately straining and relaxing as the sun set, its beauty enhanced by the suddenly still air. Insects I hadn't seen for three months—dragonflies, grasshoppers, and sand flies—buzzed around me. My mind surveyed the terrain over which we had struggled and conquered. Now I could turn my sights to the city of Santiago just 281 miles away on good concrete road. This place, which had been a goal for so long, was now almost a reality, and I found it hard to believe that I was nearly there. The scene was fresh and one to be enjoyed, rightly so, by a man who had proudly beaten the southern trail. And I did enjoy the breeze, the sun, and the shade—

without so much as a thought of thanks to God who had put it together.

Our first day back on the road, we could practically smell Santiago. In that city lay three months' mail, dehydrated food from New Zealand, and equipment sent ahead by us from Punta Arenas. We maintained a sharp pace so we could reach the city's outer suburbs in four and a half days.

March 11, my twenty-second birthday, Santiago was ours after 2,600 windblown Patagonian miles. No man could ever wish for a better birthday present than the completion of our first stage to Alaska. Now we would relax and live a civilized, normal existence for a couple of months. We pushed through the noonday crowds of Santiago's alemeda, a public walk shaded with trees, to find the British Embassy. Greetings and congratulations were showered on us from the consulate staff, who were only too glad to rid themselves of piles of mail. After several hours reading in a small café, we rode through the congested streets to the address of a house made available to us by a German family.

We were to make Santiago our base for nearly four months. Ahead lay the hot, blistering sands of the Atacama Desert; however, time and finances would permit Ian and me to see a large portion of the eastern and northeastern side of the South American continent before tackling this part of our tour. John, who had left New Zealand with less money than Ian or I, had been plagued with costly rear wheel fractures during our trip so far. He was unable to spend a further $450 to see other parts of South America without jeopardizing his participation in the rest of the cycling trip. He decided to tutor Spanish-speaking students in English while Ian and I were gone. With this in mind, he made himself available at a university-level institution and prepared to meet and make new friends while his cycling companions meandered. With regret Ian and I left him with our bicycles in Santiago and crossed the Andes back into Argentina by car.

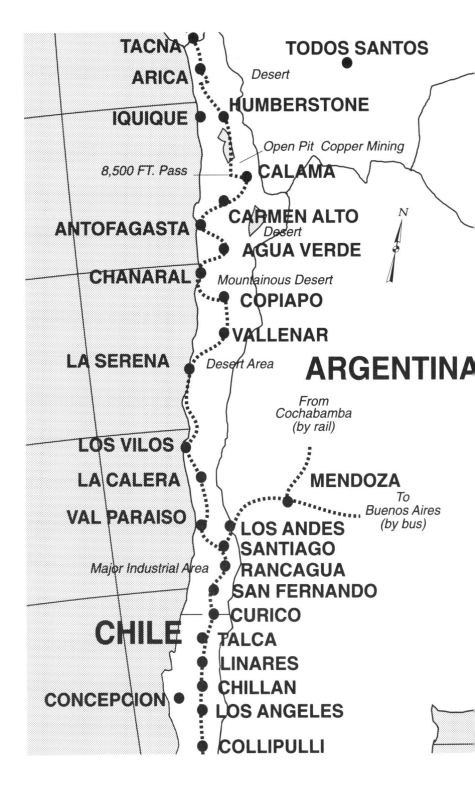

▲▼▲

5

Eastern Odyssey

A side trip to Argentina, Uruguay,
Paraguay, Brazil, and Bolivia

The sensation of a speeding car was a thrill after having traveled under our own leg power. Soon high above the small outcrops of houses, we burst through tunnels and wound around banked curves. The atmosphere grew colder as we reached the Chilean check point in the Andes some 12,000 feet above sea level. Our passports were stamped, along with those of the other occupants of the car, and we continued upward to the narrow tunnel that would take us to the other side of the Andes in Argentina.

With lights flickering on either side, we drove into the blackness of the mountain tunnel. The roadway was rutted and broken, making progress bad for the suspension and the passengers, but our Chilean driver seemed oblivious to the punishing treatment. The bumping and clanging of metal continued as we approached the speck of white light shining in the distance.

There before us stretched green, vast, central Argentina. At our backs stood the Argentine mountains. Before us the panorama lay unobstructed, obscured only by a gray haze miles and miles away. As I gazed on this magnificent sight, I felt that I could almost see the other side of the world. At a height of 14,000 feet the land lay flat, taking on the appearance of a rich, full carpet of cultivation, agriculture, and development. What a striking contrast to the barrenness of Patagonia! This was the cattle-raising area of Argentina that we had heard about in New Zealand and that I had wanted to see. This was Argentina!

The air was still cold as we checked in at the official immigration point for passport stamps and baggage and vehicle checks. Laboring buses polluted the roadside air as they slowly made their way toward us over steep grades and through rarefied atmosphere. Our descent was sudden and short. Within half an hour we approached the small border town of Mendoza where we would spend one night before bussing to the capital, Buenos Aires.

The rumble of our empty stomachs demanded instant attention, so, once cleared through immigration, we found our way to the first beefy-looking restaurant. Anticipation shone on our tanned faces as we scanned the menu, stopped at *steaks*, and commenced to order.

The waiter spoke hastily when he saw our interest. "Señor, no steaks," he muttered beneath dark eyebrows and a trimmed moustache.

"No steaks?" came my quizzical reply, glancing toward an equally disappointed Ian.

"No, señor, no steaks. Porque—pero—sin—una semana en viernes. Lo siento mucho, señor."

"Well, they haven't got'em, have they?" Ian replied, dejectedly.

"I wonder if the Paraguayans rustled all their beef? Maybe every head between the River Plate and Chile died. Or maybe the president had a dinner party. What'll we order?"

"Stick to rice and chicken, Gary. It's cheap enough," comforted Ian.

"OK, that'll have to do, I guess," I answered. "To think that Argentina is among the largest beef-producing countries in the world, and here they are rationing the stuff." I motioned to the waiter. "Arroz y pollo," I said, "con pan tambien y café (with bread and coffee, also)."

My Spanish was almost unrecognizable but soon our waiter returned with rice, chicken, and bread, and later, with black, unsweetened coffee. I recoiled at the sight and covered the white grains of rice liberally with sauce. The black coffee burned the back of my tender throat. We paid a fifteen-peso check and left, seeking the bus company that would take us to Buenos Aires.

A gray mist clung to the high-rise buildings in the heart of Buenos Aires as we arrived. The air chilled our faces as we stepped, still half asleep, from the bus. It had taken seventeen hours of nonstop traveling to reach it, but now we were on the eastern edge of the South American continent, more than 1,116 miles from John in Santiago. We had the address of two German girls we had met in Tierra del Fuego;

finding them was our next task, as they had offered us a place to stay.

After much effort, Ian and I finally arrived at the front entrance of a large apartment building. Dropping our one and only backpack of eighty pounds, we inquired about the whereabouts of our hostess. She had been expecting us and, once we located her, she immediately turned her penthouse over to us for as long as we wanted. We hadn't expected this reception and were flabbergasted. Needless to say, our stay in Buenos Aires was great. We enjoyed making many new friends and experienced the new culture, new sights, and new climate.

We heard various tales about Montevideo, the capital of little Uruguay. A steamer left Buenos Aires at 5:30 P.M. daily and arrived early the next day in Montevideo. Ian and I decided that it was too close for us to miss seeing, so off we went. After Buenos Aires, a city of four million people, Montevideo seemed dull and dirty. Broken, tumbledown buildings lined the narrow cobbled streets. Old vehicles, old buses, and old wagons jockeyed for road space. Exhaust fumes from badly tuned motors polluted the air. Pedestrians struggled past garbage cans, street lights, and drains. In one day we saw most of the city, from port to presidential palace, from stadium to parliament. We were tired as we headed back to our steamer. The voyage back was uneventful, time-consuming, and monotonous. We hurried to our private, prepaid, furnished, stocked penthouse to relax.

We had both set our sights on the Amazon River and resolved now to see it. As I stood beside the dining room table looking down at the map of South America, I contemplated different routes for our intended tour of Paraguay, Brazil, and Bolivia. Suddenly, I was aware of the vastness of our side trip. As a young man of twenty-two, I could with the line of a pen decide to see any one of a hundred cities in South America. We had money, time, and energy. I realized I was extremely fortunate to have the opportunity to do such tremendous things, to see so many different ways of life, to visit so many countries and climates.

Five days after arriving back in Buenos Aires, we regretfully left our sanctuary and bused to Asuncion, Paraguay. Here we had the first real taste of tropical life and humidity. Instead of flat, dark soil, we saw reddish clay covered with thick grass and bamboo. Tall, heavy-limbed trees burst into prominence everywhere as we traversed an ever-deteriorating road. Women, sometimes no more than girls, carried water on their heads. Standing elegantly upright, they balanced ten-gallon cans over long distances. Clothes were no longer tailored but hung loose and patched over lean, brown bodies. Children were pot-bellied and listless, encouraged to run naked in the heat of the tropical climate. I could see from the prominence of street-corner beggars and shoeshine boys that this small country was underdeveloped in almost every way.

Once more we toured a country's capital in a day and soon left for the famous Iguaçú Falls on the Brazilian border. Through tropical rain forests we traveled, seeing wildlife nip away right and left from the roadside. Slowly my system became accustomed to the choking, sticky heat of this region. Sitting for prolonged periods in buses with no air conditioning did not lend itself to comfort, but rather to prickly heat.

With border formalities completed, we crossed into Brazil, the largest country in South America. Power was one thing I noticed immediately, for the border patrol looked efficient and well armed. The radiant blackness of a Brazilian startled me. He was a big, well built man with shining muscles, more than made for jungle warfare. With an automatic rifle slung loosely over one shoulder, cigarette in his left hand, he glared unblinking at the strange assortment clambering from the stifling Brazilian bus.

I would find out later that he was typical of this country's citizens, strong in body and features. He probably was a fair guy, provided you acted as he expected.

On a tar-sealed road our bus made better time, and in a short while we had come to the small village of Iguaçú. Rusting iron overlapped in strips formed the unstable roofs of the small dwellings that dotted the streets. Thatching filled in the rotting sections. Around us, as we stepped onto the only concrete slab in the entire village, lay a sea of reddish brown mud, made worse by a recent downpour. Children and animals alike slid along beside the dwellings. Saving the weighty pack from a dunking, I lifted it carefully to the concrete while Ian asked around to find out how to get to the falls.

It would be just our luck if the spectacular falls we've come to see aren't here, I thought. Sure enough, when Ian returned, the usual smile on his face, he reported that the falls were another twelve miles down the road. If we didn't hop back on the bus in a hurry we'd miss it; and if this comedy of errors didn't cease shortly, he'd go berserk! I agreed with him; this run of events was starting to frustrate me also.

62

▲▼▲

We were asked to pay another $2.00 for the extra twelve miles, even though "Destination-Iguaçú Falls" was clearly printed on our bus ticket. When we pointed this out in Spanish to the driver, he quietly looked at us and replied in Portuguese. "Oh, no," I groaned. "This whole country, the biggest around, speaks Portuguese. Now communication is impossible."

Two dollars lighter and twelve miles sorer, we squealed to a halt outside the expensively styled Hotel de Iguaçú. Well-cared gardens and plants decorated the broad entrance, and anxious porters grinned in anticipation. Ian and I left the entrance and trudged down the concrete road with our pack to take our first look at the falls, and then to select a site for our two-night stay.

Thousands of gallons of water cascaded down, dashing onto slippery rocks, bursting and breaking, splashing and foaming, exploding and falling. This was the unique beauty of Iguaçú. Low steaming jungle, squawking birds, and money-spending tourists formed a backdrop to its power. Small tiered pathways cut a narrow way between rock and cliff, inching closer and closer to the deafening sound of falling brown water which seemed to hang suspended in midair for a fraction of a second, turn white and clear, then collide with rock to burst and froth away. Finally released and spent, with its surface glassy, it smoothed, grew fatter and slower, and joined the other rivers running to the Atlantic. These were the remarkable Cataratas del Iguaçú, shared by Argentina, Paraguay, and Brazil.

Next stop on our journey would be Rio de Janiero, the magnificent city renowned the world over both for its exotic setting and for its culture. To reach it we spent several days on large modern buses, enduring the heat, bus changes, and inaccurate timetables. Finally, accompanied by heavy rain that flooded the streets with several inches of water, we pulled into a modern depot in the old center of Rio.

Rio sprawled in every direction, encompassing hills and mountainsides, then rolling down to Copacabana Beach and to the Sugar Loaf. The majestic statue of Christ stood prominently on the sharpest pinnacle, surveying the vast former capital of Brazil; we made it our first point of sightseeing. The worn flights of concrete steps led us up to a commanding view of the ranging city. Heavy clouds shrouded the neighboring bluffs as we took picture after picture. The gray statue stood a glorious 133 feet high, and with both arms stretched out it gave

▲▼▲

the impression of a keeper looking after his charges. Tourists clamored and jostled for the best camera views, then rejoined the cable car and descended to lower levels where the rain clouds blotted out further chances for photographs.

We clanked and banged our way down, perched on hard wooden seats, disembarked, then walked over to the famous beach of Copacabana. Here the heavy Atlantic surf surged and receded in rhythmic pulsations. The late afternoon sun glittered off the water, reflecting rich color as Ian and I sat watching. People passed by; we enjoyed the sights and sounds around us. The atmosphere was different in this city; it was peculiar to Rio alone. This place had all, and more, than either of us could have asked for. With regret we turned our eyes toward the newly constructed capital of Brasília.

Along with several hours of night riding came rutted roads, uneven grades, and insects as we traveled inland from Rio. Pink tinged dawn was greeting us when we caught our first glimpse of the unusually sparse growth of Brasília's surroundings. Then we saw the glistening white buildings as they shone out from the valley. The city was built with expansion, mobility, and accessibility in mind. The roadways were now five or six lanes wide, making pedestrian life hazardous. Cars screamed along the beautiful roads, and the fast buses maintained a never-ending procession to the terminal.

Our sightseeing trip of Brasília took two days. We marveled at the design and elegance of the modern architecture. Most of the country's reserves had been used in building this world pacesetter, with all the material flown in for construction. The city was only eleven years old, so the process of transferring business from Rio was yet to be completed.

Next on our trip, 1,426 miles north, lay the city of Belém situated at the Amazon Delta. We knew this would bring us as near to the equator as we could come on the tour. We both wanted to see just what the mighty Amazon River had to offer. Without match in volume in the entire world, it flows from a glacier in the Peruvian Andes into the sweltering heat of the Amazonian Basin. The second longest river in the world, exceeded only by the Nile, its discharge can be detected 200 miles out in the salt waters of the Atlantic.

For three days we bounced around in Brazilian buses over heavily rutted mud roads, dodging quagmires and anteaters. The country soon changed from light tropical brush to thick jungle. The humidity increased and made us sticky and uncomfortable. The familiar sight of naked Indian children and fallen, dilapidated adobe huts grew monotonous as we progressed. We were entering a different way of Brazilian life and culture. No longer were there concrete and steel structures, but poverty and sickness in the eyes of the young, and dejection in the eyes of the elders. These simple people, living as they had for decades, were far removed from the bustling cosmopolitan centers of their prospering country.

To our surprise and delight, Belém was a far bigger place than we had anticipated. It stretched around the Amazon outlet, stopping abruptly at the water's edge where lines of poorly maintained boats lay. At the waterfront we jostled for a position to board a riverboat to journey 1,000 miles up the Amazon to Manaus.

Amid the confusion on board we made our way onto the lower deck of the *Laura Sobre*. Nationals had already claimed hammock sites and glared at us when we spread out our sleeping bags beneath them.

"The next several hours are going to be great," stated Ian, sprawled out on the wooden deck.

"Sure, sure," was my reserved reply as I noticed pregnant women by the score and dozens of half-naked children.

Late that same evening we left Belém for Manaus, about five days away. The twinkling harbor lights of the Belém docks soon faded, finally vanishing from view. Night life on the boat never really stopped that sticky May evening. Brazilians spat on the deck, children screamed at an ear-piercing level, and animals squawked in their new habitat.

The refuse of both animal and human habitation grew steadily worse in the ensuing days. The Brazilians lost more and more of their temporary sophistication to become grossly primitive and crude. The deck was covered with food scraps, wine, animal droppings, and human saliva. The stench grew in the Amazonian swelter. Babies cried, were breast fed, then slept until their bellies stirred them again. Not twenty feet from us at the stern of the boat were the latrines. Ducks, fowl, parrots, and other birds were tied to piping and marine tackle, while littered around them were the food morsels that passengers had thrown them. They slopped and slid through the waste to reach their food, and I felt uncomfortable as I sat and watched.

▲▼▲

We, like the livestock, were constantly being stepped on, spat on, tripped over, laughed at, and sometimes insulted. I sat nestled in the folds of my sleeping bag, taking in the scene before me. I found it hard to believe that people could exist in such close and unhealthy conditions. From my pack I withdrew my daily log and pen to try to describe the scene. This is what I wrote on the evening of May 11, our fourth day on the brown Amazon:

> 8:40 P.M. We have sat outside of Santarem for the duration of the day, while passengers have disembarked and joined us. We managed to get rid of several fellow passengers, but unfortunately we acquired more and more screaming kids and pregnant women. People here are incredibly dirty; mothers lower their babies from the hammocks to allow them to excrete on the floor rather than take them to the toilets. It is not uncommon for them to urinate in the hammocks, and after two days the stench is putrid. I have picked up a stomach bug somewhere on this germ-ridden, urine-soaked hulk. My gut grinds and I lack all energy and motivation.

On the sixth day of our voyage my intestinal problem worsened to such a degree that eating was impossible. My entire day was spent lying full length on the stinking deck amid the smell and disease, rushing to the latrines and then collapsing again.

To my delight, Manaus appeared on the eighth day. We packed hurriedly, eager to rid ourselves of the diet of rice and beans, for that is all they had fed us the entire journey. Manaus, halfway up the Amazon, had once throbbed with activity stimulated by the rubber boom. Now it lay crumbling, sufficing as an outlet for other less important exports taken to all corners of Europe. Here on the floating docks, made necessary because of the massive seasonal changes in water level, cargo was loaded and unloaded with the beautiful, simple efficiency that only Latin Americans seem to manage. Narrow streets wound and crept into the small corners of this isolated port. Row upon row of small river craft rocked gently beside one another in the flotsam of the harbor life. Beggars and poor rubbed shoulders, picked pockets, and begged for a cruzeiro or two.

After twelve days of searching for a small boat to take us to Porto

Velho, we finally found one and jumped aboard for our next water-filled miles.

The river was clearing now as we chugged deeper into the state of Mato Grosso. Here we saw snakes, crocodiles, parrots, monkeys, lizards, and almost every variety of bird, butterfly, and mammal. The Bolivian border, we anticipated, was really close and we would soon reach Guayara-mirim, the border village. We crossed the border and once again traveled for ten days by riverboat to the upper reaches of the Mamoré River to disembark from the *Angelina* and ride by banana truck into Cochabamba.

After nearly six weeks on the stifling river systems, climbing to more than a 15,000-foot elevation in a truck was a terrific shock to our systems. The road was steep and sharp; the truck lurched and rolled, giving us a true feeling of togetherness with the bananas. Chilled to the bone and scarcely able to move, we arrived in Cochabamba on the Bolivian altiplano (plateau) on June 26. This side trip had already taken longer than expected because of the 2,000 miles of slow river travel. We knew all too well that the next challenge, once back on our cycle trip, was the 3,000-mile stretch of Atacama Desert north of Santiago. If we messed around too much longer, it would mean facing temperatures upward of 120 degrees in the desert summer. That was not to be desired! Naturally, we wished to ride it in the most favorable time of year.

It was with these thoughts in mind that our journey back, south from Cochabamba through northwest Argentina, was completed by train. High on the Bolivian altiplano we were able to experience the unusual culture of the South American Indian and see him in his natural setting. Temperatures remained cool, but eventually our blood thickened sufficiently to enable us to withstand them. The clackety-clack of steel upon steel sped us into Argentina, deeper and deeper south, into the snowy Andean foothills and finally to the familiar border town of Mendoza. Our side trip had taken three months, but our chins still dropped several inches when we were told by the charming receptionist that the pass into Chile had been snowfilled for a week.

"Well, it's snowbound, sport, and that's it," I said as I checked in with my worried-looking companion.

"It is, eh? Hm, OK. Then the only alternative is to fly, I suppose," Ian said.

▲▼▲

The people were only too happy to refund our prepaid train fare—in Argentinian pesos, of course—and we left them to find at the airline office that just two seats were available on the next day's flight. With tickets tucked safely away, we spent our last night in Argentina outside the railroad station.

The next day our plane spiraled high above the favored ski fields of Mendoza. Aconcagua, the highest mountain in South America and the Western Hemisphere, radiated its splendor at 22,834 feet. Deep crags and glistening buttresses characterized the beauty of the Andean jump. With ears popping and cameras clicking, we descended into Chile. Santiago appeared bleak and chilled under a new blanket of frost and ice.

Since leaving Chile three months ago we had seen the sights of eastern South America and voyaged along huge rivers and insignificant tributaries, all in quest of adventure and experience. We now had all that behind us. What lay ahead would be more quelling and energy-sapping than we could imagine.

As we entered Santiago we wondered if John would be there or if three months had been too long for him to wait for us. Would he have left, dropped out, become uninterested in the cycling adventure?

Back in our one-room den were more dehydrated foods from New Zealand, but no John. To our relief, we learned he had ridden out to a friend's place to relax and await our return. We got in touch with him and talked over just about everything. Then Ian and I flew to Easter Island for two weeks. When we returned, we'd begin our long awaited attack on the Atacama Desert.

The season would be just right, although we expected temperatures to be high. Each had his own thoughts about how he would stand up to the heat and lack of water. In the sand-filled miles that lay before us, we would each gain new insight into our own abilities. Our struggle with northern Chile was about to begin.

▲▼▲

6

The Atacama Desert

North through Chile

The desert grit soon found its way into every article we possessed. After only sixty short miles, the sand, small rock chips, and dust filled our clothing, cooking equipment, and sleeping bags. Our once smooth-running bicycles now crunched and snapped from accelerated wear and lack of sufficient lubricant. Dust clung like some organic moss, blotting out the bright bands of color on our bars.

Since we were suffering the effects of a four-month layoff, the desert seemed especially stifling. It is the home of the Chilean condor, a huge bird with a wingspan of ten to twelve feet. It perched on high crags and danced on burning sands near the shimmering Pan-American Highway. Always in pairs or groups, they made spectacular flight patterns as they gracefully rode the warm air currents of this barren land. We also noticed the distant shuffling of the desert fox, a nomadic scavenger. These unattractive, bushy-tailed creatures robbed the food offerings placed at roadside graves. Time and time again we sneaked up on some unsuspecting animal while he was emptying a family memorial.

"How would you like to spend eternity here, John?" I asked.

"Not if I can help it, laddy," he shot back as his back tire narrowly missed touching mine.

"Watch it, John. I don't want another spill like yesterday's!" I warned.

John chuckled as he remembered the episode. Until now we had never reached an average of eighteen miles per hour. This speed, along with full loads and heat, reduced our maneuverability and reaction time. The day before, John had overcorrected and a crash had resulted.

▲▼▲

None of us was hurt, but for a short while we increased the riding distance between us until we had adjusted to the speed.

The highway twisted and fell as it meandered north along the Pacific coast as far as the city of La Serena. Then it subtly began to straighten and flatten. Before us now lay the smell of soft tar, the baking sun, and nature's own abrasive, sand.

Huge power pylons seemed to stack themselves one on top of another in a straight line and then distort and disintegrate in the shimmer of the heat. The same effect was visible as I looked forward along our road. It was laced with heat waves; mirages appeared on its surface and dissipated into fuzzy nothingness. To the right and left of us stretched miles of brown, gray, pink, and bluish sand. Hills, flats, and mountains, beautiful in their own barren way, covered the landscape, all with the same characteristic: choking sand!

The battle we faced was hard on equipment and flesh. At temperatures upward of 95 degrees, the well-packed bearing races and hubs soon became dry and noisy. The bicycles that rode silently out of the Santiago suburbs now clanked and groaned, making every revolution painful to the ears. We knew just how far this set of new gears had to carry us: into Lima some 2,000 miles away. The first days were spent painstakingly removing the worst grit from chains and sprockets, only to have them badly soiled again the next day. The desert wind was unrelenting as it blew particles of sand straight into newly oiled equipment. Chains jumped, grabbed, and jumped again as they desperately tried to maintain equal pulling power on each new tooth. After several minutes of this, they would finally settle into a routine, a little noisier but running properly.

"Whose turn to cook tonight?" Ian asked dryly, sipping from one of the half-gallon canteens.

"Yours!" said John, removing a full pint water bottle from his bicycle frame.

"That's what I figured." He smiled, smacking the cork back hard into place.

It was now 4:15 P.M., I noticed as we mounted again, having agreed to ride for a further six miles before calling it a day. This final half hour's effort would bring up our average daily mileage by three miles, making us happy at fifty-six miles for the day. In the cool that would soon turn to a chill, we quietly covered the extra six miles.

▲▼▲

The sweat that had flowed from our tanned bodies now clung and smelled. My red T-shirt crumpled as I removed it from my back to lay it across a warm rock before I relaxed. Crusted salt lined and filled my dark eyebrows. This same sweat during the day had coursed down my forehead and run unopposed into the corners of my eyes. Smarting and stinging, they blinked, clearing for a moment until a fresh deluge came from above. Every article of clothing I wore reeked with stale sweat. Washing and bathing were impossible when all available water was needed for cooking and drinking.

Standing naked except for a pair of briefs, I surveyed the changing of the day spread before me. It was my turn to pitch our tent, which gave me an opportunity to enjoy the setting of a glowing pink Atacama sun. John and Ian were preparing the two half-pint Primus stoves, peeling our last potatoes, and carefully measuring the correct amount of water for the dehydrated food.

"Hey, look at that! Isn't it beautiful, lovely, wonderful, and all sorts of good!" I shouted.

They both turned, perfectly together, and snap, I had them on film. With the steaming pot on one Primus, John measuring water, and the tent to the right on the flattest bit of ground around, the picture looked perfect against the backdrop of the sun's golden reflection on the desert landscape. These barren hills and mountains represented the entire financial resource of Chile. If they hadn't yielded vast quantities of copper, oil, and nitrate, the country could not have survived economically. It depended heavily on its mineral wealth; of copper alone it exported 99 percent of all it mined.

To the west we could see the edge of the cloud cover that makes the extreme coastal strip bearable. Here the great Humbolt Current sweeps northward, bringing with it this cooling protective cover. It continues on into Peru before swinging out into the Pacific just after the Ecuadorian border. The cloud cover stops abruptly about thirty-one miles inland where we were now situated.

In a final radiant blaze, the shimmering sun left us for another twelve hours to drop beneath the Pacific horizon. Under the gray of approaching night, we sat, supported by bags and rocks, to partake eagerly of the prepared evening meal. With fifty-six miles behind us, our stomachs growled and our mouths cracked. Taking a sip of our precious water was the only way we could manage what was on our aluminum plates. Our bodies were racked from constant exertion and dehydration. The corners of my eyes were red and sore. It grew difficult to open my mouth as my lips were cracked and often bled, but our faces and legs looked tanned and healthy as we sat on the cool sand.

Around our compact campsite lay rocks and boulders of all shapes and sizes. They, like the desert sunset air, cooled quickly. It was amazing just how quickly the temperature had changed. At one o'clock the mess cans had been too hot to handle, our tire pressure had to be released, and our 531 tubing was warm. Now, only four hours later, the plates were cold to the touch, our tires were slack and would need air, and our bicycles were leaning together lifeless and chilled. The appearance of three "desert rats" had also taken a marked change. Instead of shirts and shorts, we were now clad in long trousers, shirts, jerseys, and windbreakers to fight the evening chill.

Our hunger satisfied, we carefully measured the exact amount of water required to wash only the plates. It hurt us to see the water used this way, but we felt it was better for our health to at least try to keep things clean.

"One last sip," said John, reaching for the half-full canteen.

"OK, but make it small," Ian replied while packing away a stove. Only one stove would be necessary for our breakfast of oatmeal and sweetened black tea.

"After you, John-o," I yelled from about fifteen feet, rustling through my left pannier to find my diary.

John lowered the canteen, corked it, and propped it against a nearby rock.

"Found it," I said, holding high my notebook. "Now where in the whole Atacama is my Chilean ball point?"

"I've got it," said a smiling John, looking up from his day's entry.

"Oh, you have, have you? How's a man to fill in his daily findings? With his toenail?" I teased.

"I'll hand it over in a while."

"Oh, you will, will ya! What am I supposed to do until then? Count the hairs on the sole of my left foot?" I charged, wanting a bite from John.

"Just a minute!" he retorted, trying hard to concentrate on his last sentences.

"A fella carts a Chilean ball-point from Santiago 310 miles into this

desert, and now he can't even use it!" I pushed a little harder.

"OK, OK. Here it is then. I finished!" yelled John as he tossed it my way.

"Thanks. Now let's see. First, fifty-six miles for the day," I mumbled.

John folded up his gear, stashed it away, and headed for his sleeping bag. Ian had just finished packing the stove and was preparing for John to take over cooking duties in the morning. The lack of light prevented me from completing my entry. Under the moonlight that now bathed the lonely landscape I slipped off my clothing, took a last look at the galaxies above, and wiggled into my bag alongside the others. The tent we were using was a two-man mountain tent, but with skillful maneuvering the three of us could sleep reasonably well in it. In the present coolness of the night the closeness of others was a help, but we knew this situation would soon become unbearable when we reached the tropics.

The awareness of thirst was upon us all as we lay snug in that tent. Three men who had sweated profusely for almost twelve hours and had not replenished their dehydrated systems in full or even half measure needed more water. Outside the tent, not more than twenty feet away, nestled against a rock, lay barely enough water to give us breakfast. The water, I knew, was now deliciously cool and refreshing, so different from what we had drunk before. It was our total supply, only one and a half gallons. The next water stop was the small town, Agua Verde, just a few days from Calama, our rest stop. With fire burning hot at my chapped lips and dry tongue, I slowly fell into a deep sleep.

The next thing I knew I was awake, licking at a fresh trickle of blood from cracks at the corners of my mouth. I was hot, dehydrated, and thirsty. My face burned from excess sun, and crusted salt stuck to the jersey I had formed into a pillow. Everything suddenly seemed unbearable inside the confines of the tent. Wriggling my way clear of John and Ian, I unzipped the mosquito net and crawled out into the stillness. The blast of cool air was like snow in the tropics; it sent shivers up and down my spine. Now I shook as I gazed upward. The clearness of the night was breathtaking. The surrounding hills and flats were bathed by a bluish moon glow that transformed it back into daylight. I walked to where the water and stove lay, eyed them, then went on, picking my path through the sharp desert gravel.

▲▼▲

I noticed fresh tracks I hadn't seen before. They looked like they might be from a desert fox. I followed them a brief distance, then decided I felt cold enough to return and try to get more sleep. My watch read 2:15 A.M. as I wriggled back into my bag and promptly dropped into oblivion, still thirsty.

At dawn's first light, I felt John stir, yawn, and strike out. I estimated it was 5:00 A.M.

"See you in a quarter of an hour," he said as he stumbled out only half awake.

"You're crazy," I yawned back at him.

We both knew if we didn't get moving soon, old man Sol would catch us and take the sting out of our pace.

John felt the terrain and heat far more than either Ian or I. Now, he'd push things along so we could move out quickly. This enabled us to cover the most miles during the morning before being forced to stop at 11:30 A.M. by the blazing heat.

The oatmeal was already half cooked when I greeted John and started mixing our ration of powdered milk. Quickly now, Ian emerged, folding the sleeping bags, and within minutes was packing the lightweight tent. Inside thirty minutes our camp was demolished and breakfast was being eaten. Our thirst was fierce as we completed the bowl of sticky porridge and waited patiently for a cup of tea.

Stacking dirty dishes inside his right-hand pannier, John turned to me and asked the time.

"5:45 A.M.—early." I stopped and swallowed the last mouthful of tea.

"Fine," said John, heading for the last bag to be packed and loaded.

With heavy gulps of fresh, clear air, we whisked our way along the bumpy hard-top road and felt the tired muscles of yesterday's work. Ahead of us lay a week's rest and better food but, above all, the pleasure of New Zealand hospitality.

A Salvation Army corps from New Zealand worked in the district of Calama, a few minutes' drive from the world's largest opencast copper mine, Chuquicamata. Badly dehydrated and wishing nothing more than to become clean again, we rolled into the camp and located our New Zealand friends. They greeted us with friendship and open house. We had intended to rest at this point and that's exactly what we did. We enjoyed the discussions, which covered all kinds of subjects. We could only admire this couple for their dedication and call against immense adversity.

For one short week we remained within those friendly walls. Finally it was time to depart as the journey pressed.

The climb up to the pass above the Chuquicamata mine was heavy hauling after a week's layoff. The terrain was similar to what had preceded, and our routine slid back into place. But now we faced each day a little fresher. This freshness would last about three days, and then, as usual, the sun and travel conditions would wear us down. Even at this point, only 9,000 feet above sea level (our highest point so far), our lungs felt the lack of oxygen.

Gasping, we reached the neck of the pass and took five minutes to absorb the view.

"I have a flat!" I shouted over my shoulder to Ian and John.

"Oh well, we can sit here and admire the view a little while longer while you repair, Gary," beamed Ian.

"Guess so," I said as I rested my bike upside down against a large boulder. "Where's the booting material? I need to resleeve this split if I want the last few miles from this tire," I asked, trying to speed up the process.

"In my back right pannier pocket," Ian answered, tossing a rock in the direction of a terrified lizard.

The entire process of taking off, repairing, and replacing the tire took only about fifteen minutes.

"What in the world took you so long?" teased John. It was a bad time for a joke. With rivers of sweat running down my sunburned face, I looked at him and glared. Hiding the smirk that threatened to escape my lips, I mounted and onward we rolled over a perfect, straight, heat-softened road.

One day we caught sight of an irrigation reservoir, shimmering in the midafternoon heat, shaded by green willows, just visible to the squinting naked eye. Since we had already covered close to forty-three miles that day, an early stop where we had water, shade, and grass was welcome. The setting was soothing and peaceful to the heart. Inside the encircling willows, even our eyes could rest from the constant sand glare; the soft flow of running water between the moss banks refreshed our nerves.

▲▼▲

The opportunity to completely submerge and scrub our grimy, smelly bodies was a special kind of relaxation. Our last wash of any description had been five days earlier in a similar irrigation ditch. This was typical of our desert existence. When circumstances permitted, we washed, but all too frequently, we remained sweat-ridden for days. Our total water carrying capacity, specifically for desert survival, was twenty-four precious pints. This gave sufficient cooking allowance if we rationed it correctly. It did not allow for any waste, the extravagance of bathing, or the proper quenching of a deep and fierce thirst.

However, in this unaccustomed oasis, I could forget about all these things. I could bathe, wash a rotting set of cycling clothing, and drink cool water, pumped directly from the ground, as much as I wanted. Ahead lay several large commercially exploited salt lakes; tomorrow would see us well into this region. In an effort to balance our bodies' water content, we drank as if water were going out of style.

The afternoon's activities passed in a fury of washing, bathing, and drinking tea. When we had consumed one pot of the dark brown liquid, we wasted no time placing another on the Primus. The light faded slowly, suddenly disappearing behind a desert mountain range. Once again we were bathed in lunar glow.

Inside a week we arrived at Chile's most northern town, Arica. Reaching Arica signaled an end to the first stage of the Santiago to Lima leg, and it was hard to immediately realize our accomplishment. We were only about halfway through the Atacama, but once in Peru we would ascend into the Andes, leaving the intense coastal heat. Our bodies had suffered enough from prolonged sun and dehydration.

We were challenged by the thought of traveling high into the Peruvian Andes to Lake Titicaca and Machu Picchu. This appealed to our sandblasted minds far more than riding the scorching miles from the border to Lima. On studying the only Peruvian map we possessed, we found that this sojourn into the mountains and altiplano would tack another 558 miles onto the second stage of our Santiago to Lima leg.

Looking ahead to the more picturesque scenery we knew we would encounter deep in the Andes, we hurried through border formalities and headed along the Pan American Highway to the beautiful southern Peruvian region of Tacna. A little over 1,240 miles of desert, numerous broken spokes, and countless tire punctures were behind us.

▲▼▲

At Tacna, John changed to a steel rim and spokes for his rear wheel. Throughout our desert journey, he had been plagued with snapped spokes. Already he had gone through three wheels while Ian and I each had changed one. The light alloy rims served both Ian and me well, but John, a heavier man, was much harder on his equipment. The decision to change to steel was easy, since he now needed the strongest wheel he could purchase for the rugged mountain climbing that stretched before us; but actual construction of the wheel was full of frustration. And John had to make it to Lima on this wheel!

After we had purchased appropriate length spokes and a new rim, Ian and I started construction. We retained John's original Campagnolo hub that seemed in good enough condition to last many more miles, then threaded the spokes through machined holes in the hub, laced and crossed them. Once every spoke was in place, key ones were attached to the rim and temporarily tightened in position. At this stage the hub was off-center, making John's wheel look lopsided. As more spokes were adjusted and tightened, however, this unevenness was gradually rectified. Later we presented John with his new firmly braced steel wheel. We anticipated good results from our many hours of labor.

The final day in Tacna arrived and, escorted out of town by young Peruvian cyclists, we started on the next stage to Lima.

▲▼▲

7

Rising to the Sun

Climbing in the Andes

Towering majestically in the east were the foothills of the Andes. Purple and blue in color, they stood in the haze of the Peruvian Desert. Tacna had been an oasis to us, as had other small hamlets in the Atacama. This beautiful little town had provided a badly needed respite to the relentless, stifling desert heat. As we bicycled out, we viewed it one last time. Its small, rutted, cobbled streets interlaced block after block and converged centrally at the town's cathedral and plaza. Grass terraces bordered by colorful flowers surrounded the plaza.

Thirteen miles out, we said farewell to Tacna, the last town that would have any modern comforts. Ahead were the Indians of the altiplano and finally, on the shores of Lake Titicaca, Indians who eked out an existence floating on reed rafts. Our bodies were adjusting to the severity of climbing hills and the drastically reduced mileage. We had forgotten what it felt like to ride climbing gears all day and now had to recall that knowledge. Although in the rolling sands of the Atacama we had averaged thirteen miles per hour, now we averaged only twenty-two miles per day!

Initially, progress on the sandy, graveled road was appalling. Our newly-purchased food supplies burdened us. Deep ruts prevented deviation for fear we'd overbalance or buckle a wheel.

Doubling back and forth, we inched forward over soft, loose mountainous roadway. Since we had not yet gained enough altitude to sufficiently cool off, sweat coarsed down our faces and ran unchecked from our torsos. Leg muscles flexed, relaxed, and flexed again, push-

▲▼▲

ing us upward into the thin atmosphere. We were approaching an experience we had never encountered before.

"Next corner we stop for a break," called Ian, who always rode up front to govern our pace.

"OK, OK," came our fatigued replies from behind.

Through a sweaty haze we labored over rocks and shale to the next hairpin bend. The bike stopped suddenly once the rhythmic effort of my legs ceased. It lay heavy between my thighs as I sat astride it, almost too exhausted to dismount and sit down.

"Man, just look at the view!" admired John, reaching into his front bag for his camera.

"Yep. I guess I'll take one too," I answered, propping the heavy bicycle against the inside of the curve. We sat for ten minutes admiring the awesome mountains, chain upon chain that ceased only when they reached the Pacific Coast. This view from the back was commanding, but the one we could see by looking forward and tilting our heads was formidable. Ahead towered mountain range upon mountain range, ridge upon ridge, each fighting the others for dominance.

I mounted, kicked off, and hastily slid my right shoe into the stirrup just in time to propel myself one revolution farther into the Andes. After the first several revolutions, balance became easier as timing and effort synchronized. Too much force or energy expended at inappropriate times quickly led to exhaustion. An even, rhythmic pressure was required by both legs for my body to achieve maximum potential over the greatest distance. It was hard mastering the technique of restrained, applied effort, but once I developed it, mountain-climbing fatigue was considerably lessened. Neglect meant severe headaches, nosebleeds, and unnecessary tightness in the chest and legs.

As our dusty, potted road continued upward, we searched for a suitable site for our evening camp. Each Indian in the fertile foothills took charge of his own small plot of soil. Every scrap of land was in use. Cattle and a few bedraggled sheep grazed. The only source of water was miles above a person's farmhouse and stock.

Our altitude was now almost 7,000 feet. The evening's chill penetrated quickly. Ian and John hurriedly erected the tent as I peeled potatoes and sliced some fresh meat we'd brought from Tacna. We decided we'd better eat this Peruvian meat before it spoiled or fell out of one of our panniers. This, accompanied by a fried egg and some dehydrated

John cycles high in the snow-covered Peruvian Andes. At this point, the altitude is approximately 14,500 feet.

food, made up our evening meal. The day's efforts had been great and, although the meal filled us for a short while, the gnawing hunger soon began again. The night temperature was colder than that of the Atacama. Both Ian and John had heavier sleeping bags than I. Only by using a lightweight "space" blanket was I able to sleep warm.

The early hour of 5:00 A.M. crept around. Amid the rustle of bedding and the clanking of aluminum cans and plates, I prepared the morning's ration of oatmeal. The mountains held back the sun's early morning rays. With gloves, windbreaker and long pants on, I knelt beside the small Primus stove wishing that it, rather than the sticky oatmeal, could warm me. Ian hailed a perfunctory good morning and began to prepare the milk.

"Freeze the toes off a Laplander's foot, wouldn't it?" I joked, trying to warm our relationship as well as the porridge.

"What do you think lies ahead—more mountains?" Ian gulped and glanced in my direction. "Guess we go up a little way, then down a little way, then up again. Trouble is, we never seem to go down enough."

"That'd be dead right," I said. "How're your legs—tight?"

Ian appeared to have recovered reasonably well from the attack of diarrhea he'd had in Tacna. Although weak at first, he seemed to improve as each day passed. A man with far greater experience than either John or I, Ian was able to control his effort and ration his energy evenly over the cycling hours. He, in turn, had coached us in these finer points. We had learned well. Our legs could pump the pedals, cranks, chain rings, and gears all day without undue strain or malfunction. I thought how lucky we were to have been blessed with bodies that functioned normally.

The weakness that had once hampered my sporting activities had disappeared. When I was in my teens, my right kneecap had begun to flake, and the bone slivers would catch in the joint, causing excruciating pain. After administering heat and injections, specialists had decided to try one more treatment. If that didn't work, it would be necessary to remove my kneecap. This last attempt to save my knee required my entire right leg to be immobilized for three months. They hoped a restricting cast and lack of activity would enable the underside of the cap to heal, gloss over, and thereafter perform normally. When the plaster was removed, I exercised at the clinic for six weeks.

▲▼▲

Previously inactive muscles were finally able to operate fully without stabbing, bone-jarring pain. It worked. Even here in the Andes under constant strain, my right knee showed no sign of weakening. I was pleased to see equally sized muscles, bulging and smooth-working, in both legs.

The shadows of the previous night dispersed, taking with them the moistness and cold, and we continued our climb to Puno. Homes appeared more frequently. We passed Indians driving stock or eating meager breakfasts beside warm earthen ovens. At one sharp-crested ridge the road took a long, hairpin plunge. Below in the mist of the October morning lay the Andean town of Tarata. We had climbed continuously since leaving camp and estimated that we were now cycling at altitudes of over 10,000 feet.

In the village we purchased needed food supplies, but we pushed on as quickly as we could. The winding road rose even steeper. Within half an hour Tarata had faded from view.

Stress and fatigue came upon us quickly as we ascended to the roof of the world. Our pace slowed as our legs became heavy and our hearts throbbed noisily in our ears. My lungs and chest ached for more oxygen. I glanced behind me at John. The distance between us had lengthened. Below his nose a stream of blood trickled over the top lip into his gasping mouth. The backs of his big hands were stained with the coagulated blood he had tried to wipe away. His eyes drooped and his face was stamped with exhaustion and anguish. Ian was also in trouble, for our pace had dropped by almost half. Blood swelled in my own nose; I felt it begin to trickle slowly downward, and it soon ringed my left nostril. A rain shower caused the road to deteriorate, balancing seemed almost impossible, and exertion doubled. Our altitude was now over 13,000 feet. My lungs wanted to explode as they ached for oxygen that wasn't there.

Not able to push around the rubble on the next curve, we halted for a short while.

"You OK, John?" I asked. "Is it bad?"

"Only a nosebleed," came his hoarse reply as he sat heavily on a rock ledge.

"You sure you're OK?" questioned Ian, who was breathing extremely hard and looked whiter than either John or I.

"Yeah, just give me time to acclimatize," John asserted. "Man, look at that view. What variation of color!"

"You bleeding, Gary?" Ian asked, picking up his bike.

"Not much. Just a small leak in the left nose," I quipped, trying to be smart.

"Right. Then let's take another stab at it," Ian urged.

Breathing more evenly, we pushed off and up to the horizon—only to discover another higher crest of Andes half a day's ride away. We were still not at the top, even at an altitude of more than 13,500 feet! As usual, Ian led the way, but this time his lead was slow and faltering. He was weak and uncoordinated. I had almost closed our riding distance when he had to stop to regain his wind. Leaning heavily on the handlebars and front bag, he vomited. I gave him the remaining two altitude sickness tablets and pressed on, trying to reach a suitable campsite or the summit of a road. There wasn't a thing I could do to help him.

The thin atmosphere affected each of us differently. My own problems had only just started. Numbness crept into the depths of my heaving diaphragm; my eyes ached; my nose was full of soft, clotted blood that threatened to burst and fill my mouth. My heart was beginning to flutter; my arms, legs, and feet felt like lead. John followed behind me, and soon, exhausted, breathless, and unable to speak, we leaned against our bikes—spent. Ian, in the distance behind us, was still crumpled over his handlebars.

"We've got to ride a little farther, John," I coughed.

"We can't go too far, Gary; Ian will never catch us. Look at him. He's not even riding anymore."

I gasped my agreement. We'd stop at the next spot.

Although only 3:30 P.M., the threat of the impending night's freeze was in the air. Even the exertion of pushing uphill at almost 15,000 feet didn't keep us warm. We were wearing all our clothing, and we were still cold.

The road bent, spiraled, and then slowly dropped into a massive basin of clefts. The sun had disappeared. Our faces, feet, fingers, and ears began to grow numb. John and I wheeled our bikes off the road and hastily made a fire of the only available tinder, the dry fungus that lay around us. The temperature would be freezing that night and we both knew it; this growth was a blessing from the Lord. After we started cooking supper on the two small Primuses, we began to thaw

▲▼▲

our extremities over the moss fire. Within a quarter of an hour, Ian walked up, ghost white, short of wind, and obviously feeling awful. He wanted no food, only cupful after cupful of hot tea. He was exhibiting the symptoms of altitude sickness we had been warned of at Tacna, but he stubbornly refused to take the tablets. For some reason he was suffering far more than John or I.

It was peculiar how the thin air affected us. Movements were slower. Any exertion took minutes to recover. It seemed too much trouble to think about anything as we huddled close to the fire, soaking up all the heat we could. Our shoe leather burned while our backs remained cold.

The memory of waking up shivering on that October sixth morning will never leave me. I was cold, damp, and aching. I reluctantly climbed out of my bag and into the only article of clothing I hadn't slept in, my windbreaker, and gave myself a reorientation lecture. "Now you're 15,000 feet up, sport. It's cold; you're hungry; Ian's sick. Get him to take a tablet. And get down from this sickening height!"

Ian couldn't eat breakfast, so he left ahead of us. He wanted to cover as much ground as he could before we caught up with him. He did take the altitude tablet. John and I packed clumsily with numbed fingers. We didn't waste a motion; we didn't even have the energy to converse. We rode on, feeling lifeless and needing oxygen more than food.

Finally there it was! That pinnacle of rocks that signaled the top, 17,100 feet above sea level. The icy blast of wind made us retreat even further into our clothing. The rock pinnacle that marked the summit stood lifeless and cold. John and I stopped momentarily, numb, hearts pounding, blood throbbing in our ears, to gulp in mouthfuls of diluted oxygen; then, with a last look at the summit, we clumsily remounted to start the descent.

Downward we rode into scruffy vegetation over more bad roads, headed toward a well-earned rest at Puno, elevation 12,000 feet. It sat on the shore of the world's highest large navigable lake, Lake Titicaca.

On the third day from the top, we rode into Puno. The highland Indians spoke mostly Quechua, their native dialect. The market was bustling and colorful. People were well wrapped against the cold, but they struck me as being woefully backward in their outlook and purpose in life. Brightly colored but ragged skirts clothed the thickset, broad-faced women. The men wore patched trousers and undersized jackets. Their features were heavy, and their mouths were ringed with saliva stained green by the coca leaf, a narcotic they chewed constantly. This drug gave them warmth but promoted a lackadaisical attitude toward life. They seemed content to let the world pass them by, as long as they were able to get enough of the plant.

We pitched our faded mountain tent in a small hillside holding paddock. It offered little comfort, but held a commanding view of the lake and surrounding area.

Three days passed while we waited for Ian, who had stripped the threads from the inside of his bicycle's bottom bracket. He managed to purchase another part large enough to rerun old threads and hold adjustment.

The next rest stop on our tight schedule was to be the famous Inca ruins of Machu Picchu at 15,000 feet. It was not until the seventh day from Puno that we finally stopped at road's end, twenty-five miles from Machu Picchu. We had climbed a total of nearly 80,000 feet to this point. Now the road had ended; the only way we were going to arrive at the Inca city was by struggling up the side of the railway track. We stood on the thunderous banks of the Urubamba River that grew rapidly as it became one of the main tributaries of the mighty Amazon. Ian and I had seen the delta of the Amazon on our extended side trip through South America. Now in the depths of the Peruvian Andes, nearly 3,000 miles away from the delta, we viewed one of its sources.

The jolting, monotonous drain-hopping and railroad tie-jumping lasted three days. Finally we were able to lift our eyes to the dizzy heights of Machu Picchu—a once powerful civilization, beaten and dispersed by the conquistadors and now almost forgotten. Numerous legends told of the activities surrounding these strange people. The atmosphere generated by the ruins themselves was stirring. The panoramic view stunned me. Surrounding us were sheer rock faces, covered in light jungle growth, dropping into the Urubamba River valley. We could have stayed for weeks, walking, sitting, and taking photos, but we realized that the rainy season for this region was chasing us back to the coastal strip and Lima.

We said farewell (though I vowed to return) and set our course as directly as possible for Nasca and the Pan American Highway. Now all the altitude we had fought so hard to gain slipped beneath our worn tires. Instead of pushing, we were braking; instead of aching legs, we now experienced aching wrists and hands. Pair after pair of brake shoes wore out, shredded by uneven rims. We had become accustomed to altitudes up to 15,000 feet, so after our mammoth climb our bodies seemed to have settled in for high-altitude cycling.

Successfully passing through several police controls, we rolled off twisting, rutted soft road onto beautiful hard top at Nasca. From there, we knew our progress would be unhampered right up into Medellín, Colombia, two countries away. It was pleasant to sit in warm sun and once again experience desert nights, but we were tired and wanting our mail, good food, and a bed; so we pushed on, bent on making the 248 miles to Lima in five days.

In our anticipation, our pace quickened. The beat of muscled legs strengthened, and the hum of worn gears grew louder. The Andean trip had added 550 miles to our tour; but with the going as easy as it had become, we soon forgot those torturous days. We arrived in Lima on schedule, looking and feeling every inch the Andean champions— tanned, well muscled, and young.

We stayed three weeks, a short time in which to renew all transmission parts, build new wheels, read our waiting mail, and relax sufficiently to move north to where we intended to spend Christmas 1971, at Trujillo. This would be our second layover with a Salvation Army missionary couple, and once again it was through the dedication of these people that the Lord presented His love and purpose to us, available through His Son.

Even though we paused to celebrate the birth of Jesus, we did not really understand the meaning of the day. I acknowledged the virgin birth that had brought forth a baby named Jesus, but it was of no significance to me. December 25 was not a religious holiday for me, and I didn't celebrate it as one; yet here we were in Peru spending Christmas with a couple who were very serious and joyful about the birth of Christ. If they wanted to revere this day, or even this season, it was OK with me, although I didn't share their hope or dedication.

Reality lay in preparing for our crossing into Panama via the Darién Gap. Conversation passed between us for countless hours as we discussed problems and solutions. Our lives were dominated by this all-important topic.

After saying farewell to our friends in Trujillo, we began cycling

once again through desert sand. But subtly the passing scenery was changing. Large lumps of brownish vegetation began to appear. Soon greenery showed along the road's edge. Trees appeared, though stark and naked, looking alone and lifeless in the scorching wilderness. Our desert life of thirst, glare, and cracked lips was quickly ending. Ahead lay the humid tropical lowlands of Ecuador and the mountainous climb to Quito.

The northern Peruvian border town of Tumbes was in sharp contrast to its southern counterpart, Tacna. Instead of grass, gushing water, and flowered terraces, the market was a jumble of goods, meat, and vegetables strewn over the ground. The stench from food lying in the sun—fingered, sat on, and spat at—was quite something. Babies were breast fed, meals were eaten, and money changed hands in communal bliss.

Ecuador looked small and unimportant. We figured to cross it in five days. To our dismay we found ourselves progressing at a slower pace. We climbed for days, disappearing and reappearing in the clouds. Then we hit cobbles! Our slow progress slowed even further. We had lightly dismissed the entire mileage in Ecuador, but ten days after entering we had only just crossed the equator, viewed Ecuador's highest mountain, Chimborazo, at 20,561 feet, and arrived in Quito. Ecuador in five days! It was beyond us.

Quito clung to a mountainside. The streets snaked around antiquated dwellings. High loads were transported on the hunched backs of Ecuadorian porters. Trash covered cobbled lanes and littered shop doorways. Rain fell, spilling over cobblestones to flood and then slowly disperse.

Since Colombia was the next country, our last before the Atrato and the Darién trek, we started inquiring about equipment. Would we need hammocks? Would we need a gun? What constituted adequate medical supplies? These and many other questions confronted us. Although this stretch of the journey was still a month's ride away, it became the focus of our thoughts. We had known when we left New Zealand that the road in Colombia ceased forty miles east of the Atrato River and that there was only a projected road through the Panamanian jungles.

Our quest for answers and solutions dominated the next miles as we rode steadily into southern Colombia, eventually arriving at

Medellín. Cultivated fields clung to steeply rolling hillsides. Farmers used oxen to plant crops and haul vegetables.

Apart from some stomach problems, we arrived in reasonably good shape for the lengthy job of gathering and organizing information about what lay ahead.

The vastness of our expedition came upon me when I remembered what we had already accomplished. I had seen South America fairly thoroughly; but now, having crossed the equator, a whole new world was about to open.

Our life-style was to change dramatically, from cycling to swamp and jungle survival. My own spiritual awareness was undergoing a change, also. Before, I had blatantly rejected the significance of Jesus and even of God's material provision; now I was becoming less judgmental and a little more tolerant. The task ahead dwarfed us. In these weeks of preparation and the coming months of unprecedented struggle for survival, God was to reveal Himself to me in a wonderful way. He was to show me beyond doubt that He loves us all.

▲▼▲

8

The Ultimate Challenge

On to Medellín and El Tigre, Colombia

He was hunched backed, head sunk into aging shoulders, small in stature, and dressed in the stench and grime of tattered rags. On his head he wore a crumpled, old hat probably taken out of a trash can. He carried a wooden crutch to support his awkward progress as he shuffled past bars and restaurants begging for food. The management, or one of the customers, usually gave the beggar what he asked for so he'd go away. With fumbling hands he hungrily stuffed his mouth, making his unkempt, graying beard greasy and rice-flecked.

When he had received a handout at one place, he made his way, stumbling, along the sidewalk to the next bar to repeat his cry. In a day he could make his way unaided up and back on this one street in Envigado, a tiny town just south of Medellín. In the evening he returned to his cold corner, joining the refuse, rats, and dogs for the night. He was considered a germ, a parasite, a cyst on society; he was of no use to anybody. Yet he was a person who could know emotion just like me; he just happened to be blind and crippled. Why? I wondered.

I had seen many such people on the tour and was thankful I had been born in an advanced society and given a fit, well-muscled body. But whom should I thank? Some god or angel? Or some being who had created all the sights I had experienced? I couldn't say. All I knew was I had to thank somebody, and it wasn't me. For some time I asked myself questions but found no solutions. Why was this guy born into a life of begging, while I was given the opportunities denied him? I had been able to come and see his confined world; yet he, blind from birth, would never even see his own surroundings, let alone another country. Why was I so fortunate? It seemed to me that I had blessings beyond measure compared to this bedraggled beggar. What was his purpose in life? What hope did he have for the future?

To get to town I had walked down a very steep concrete road for a quarter mile, past a small group of shops, and over a putrid river that the nearby houses used for refuse disposal. Then walking along rutted, narrow footpaths, I passed building sites and stacks of bricks. The street was dark and in disrepair. Cars normally drove without lights or with little concern for the pedestrian. Nearer town I passed houses with doors that opened straight onto the crumbling sidewalk. Children played in doorways, nearly meeting death by automobiles. Dirty water was thrown heedlessly out into the gutter, already choked with litter, decaying food, and sludge. The stench was unbearable. I continued to walk on road and pavement until I reached the bars, restaurants, and snooker rooms.

Snooker rooms and gambling dens were filled with smoke and the deafening noise of laughter, betting, and shouting. But tables off to the side enabled a fellow to sit down and relax. A thundering juke box moaned and wailed out the local beat that never varied from record to record or, indeed, from bar to restaurant. I sat enjoying my drink and the music.

Next to me, sprawled drunkenly across a small, beer-covered table, was a man so inebriated that to move his big toe would have been a mammoth effort, if not impossible. To my right a loving couple sat enjoying the thundering jukebox, a cold bottle of fruit juice, and each other's earlobes. Before long, my ears ached from the noise, so I paid my peso bill and left the din behind. *"Make sure your hand is firmly in your pocket and on top of your wallet,"* I told myself. *"That's your restaurant over there, dimmed lights, no jukebox, and it looks clean enough. Watch that guy behind you!"*

I strolled over, took a seat, and ordered the dinner of the night for about nine pesos (fifty cents). I then settled back to wait. Finally the tired-looking waiter brought me the first course, a greasy bowl of water with a few floating vegetables and a suggestion of chicken. A glass of milk accompanied it. A little while later, he returned with the main course: a generous serving of rice plus a small slice of meat, three onion rings, half a small green tomato, and a mouthful of beans. *"What* can you expect for nine pesos? All the money is for service," I told myself. Halfway through most meals I was plagued by either shoeshine boys, ticket sellers, or deformed beggars. All asked for a dime or the scraps off my plate. This meal was no exception.

The meal over, I paid the bill and left to look for a cheap show or to just look around. I first walked up the same filthy street I had come down and checked on a show. I quickly ruled it out. It was not to my liking and entirely in Spanish. In Medellín cinemas abounded, but not so in Envigado.

Next I watched a game of snooker (pool) until my eyes and feet got tired. The next choice was obvious, more tinto (black coffee) and a serious study of a deteriorating situation. Locating another noisy bar, I wiped the beer from the seat and ordered. The music continued as I sipped at the sweetened tinto and pondered my situation.

"*Ever thought of going to midnight mass?*" I asked myself.

"*Are you crazy?*" I answered back. "*I don't mind looking at churches and admiring their beauty, but midnight mass! You've got the wrong guy!*"

From the corner of my eye I saw a gentleman in reasonably nice dress, but drunk, come stumbling toward me. Tottering, he slumped into a chair at the opposite table and grinned at me. I thought to myself, "*Finish you cola and move on!*"

"*Take a walk around the plaza and start for our camp. Seems like it's the best place to be,*" I decided, trying to console myself.

So, with hands in pockets and my head swinging from side to side to keep an eye on everything around me, I circled the litter-strewn plaza then headed up the road to my waiting jungle hammock and a night's rest. I hoped with all my strength that filth and squalor like this might never find a place in my own country.

Reaching Envigado and Medellín took the final days of our ten-month struggle with the Andes. Three mountain ranges gave us our final taste of mountain climbing and 10,000-foot atmosphere. Desperately stretching each day's effort as far as we could, we first reached the small but beautifully laid-out city of Cali. Progress had been slow through friendly patchwork-quilted mountainsides. Then the terrain changed to flat, broad, fertile valleys flanked by the towering, hazy Andean ranges.

We thought in Cali we might find answers to many of our questions about jungle travel. So, after concluding formalities at the con-

▲▼▲

sulate, we paid a call on the British consul. He faced the three of us, wishing to be congenial and helpful. Our questions came like gunfire. "Where can we purchase a good jungle hammock? What medical supplies would you recommend we take?" Umpteen others—where, what, and how—were blurted out as they came to mind.

The consul's face grew heavy as his eyebrows dropped and his mouth tightened. He cleared his throat, dragged on his pipe, adjusted his glasses, and leaned back deeper into his padded chair.

"Well, boys, as far as Cali is concerned, we're too far south to handle the specific jungle equipment you require. I suggest that you get in touch with the embassy when you reach Medellín. They will be in a better position to help you. Sorry, but merchants just don't handle that stuff here."

It was obvious that he couldn't help us, so we left his plush office more than a little disappointed. Cali had not produced the answers we were looking for; so, after a quick tour, we left it behind us.

The city of Medellín lay 285 miles north over reasonable road. It now assumed immense importance. There we had to find answers to our questions before we could enter the jungle. The entire planning and purchasing that would see us into the city of Panama would have to be done there.

For weeks we had been thinking, talking, and sleeping jungle. Our minds had already begun to make the change from cycling to packing. We burned with the challenge, hot with anticipation for the unknown. From the outset, Darién Gap had constituted the only hazardous barrier that could deny us the overland title. We were determined; to us it was almost a foregone conclusion that we would succeed. Our morale was high even if the answers we sought hadn't come at Cali. They would be found at Medellín, six days away.

Medellín is the second largest and most important city in Colombia. As usual we made our first stop the British Embassy. Here, to our surprise, a woman held the consulate position. She viewed us with interest and, I think, a certain amount of awe. Though she was gravely concerned about the trek we planned, she put herself at our service. Through her we managed to find a man with jungle experience. As I look back, I know this man was a blessing from God.

Mike had been born in England and had come to Colombia to teach at one of the many English schools. He and his family had lived there for nearly twenty years. He had varied interests in the jungle, including its orchids, tramping, and overland mapping. His information was superior to that of any book or lecture. We sat glued to our seats, soaking up everything he said. We asked every question we could think of, and Mike answered them fully and concisely. This man who knew the jungle was God's provision for us.

None of us knew much about the jungle, but after our talks with Mike, our pooled facts astounded even us. We might not have been exceptional scholars, but our knowledge had certainly improved all of a sudden. Ian, John, and I came to the same understanding: ahead of us lay country considered by many, including Mike, to be unhealthy and often dangerous. Not only did the completion of our overland cycling trip hang in the balance, but our lives as well. The more time we spent with Mike, the stronger became the urge to get in there and make our effort.

His experience guided every purchase from medical supplies to hammocks. We sat and listened like three little schoolboys fascinated by some fairy tale. However, it would be no fairy tale, but reality—the reality of survival.

Ian and I had to take a side trip by plane to Bogotá, the capital of Colombia, to purchase snake serum. Mike had stressed the number and variety of snakes in the Darién and urged us to take a broad-spectrum serum. While in Bogotá we also bought three Colombian army-issue jungle hammocks. Armed with four vials of serum, half a dozen syringes, packs, and jungle hammocks, we flew back to John. John had certainly held up the Medellín end of things: the final purchases were almost complete.

Now came the frustrating job of sorting equipment. The equipment needed for the final 217 miles of cycling from Medellín to the road's end at El Tigre was different from the equipment needed for the jungle trek from El Tigre to Panama. There were also some things we would not need until we reached Panama City. We had to pare down our pile of supplies, and the choices were not always obvious. We did not always agree on what should be taken; clear thinking did not always dominate our discussions. There were problems, troubled feelings, and arguments. This task of shedding equipment was difficult, but essential.

After three days of packing and a farewell dinner, we began our

John performs one of the trip's more tedious routines—sorting
through equipment. Packages of dehydrated food were some
of the most important supplies.

▲▼▲

last cycling miles on the South American continent. In about 217 miles we would dismantle our bikes and begin walking. After bumping and jarring our way past small jungle hamlets, we eventually reached the junction of the projected Pan American Highway that would someday traverse the great Atrato Swamp. There was a surveyed line out through the swamp as far as the Atrato River and, although it led across bad, soft-bottomed swamp, we considered it to be the shortest way to the Panamanian border. Here at this junction our walk would begin. Little did we realize it would sap the very marrow from our bones and threaten our lives.

The five thatched huts that made up the junction of El Tigre sagged, and everybody viewed our hairy, well-tanned, and muscled bodies with giggly laughs. Dogs and chickens gathered alongside the smiling children who were enthralled at the intricacies of the bicycles. They watched intently as we dismantled transmission parts from our bikes and carefully oiled each piece, wrapping it in cloth and then placing it inside several layers of plastic bags. Our unnecessary equipment pile now mounted: we would send all our cycling clothes, sleeping bags, and panniers on to Panama. Our necessary equipment consisted of hammocks, food, bikes, and dismantled parts, one change of clothing, medical kit, and cameras. These bags were heavy enough, so we had to part with everything else.

We had been given maps of the area in Medellín by the forward liaison officer for the British army's attempt to cross this same Darién Jungle. Through Captain Groves we also possessed a detailed map plotting the old survey line and giving information about the vegetation of the Atrato Swamp. This packet of precious maps also was carefully placed inside several plastic bags. Should they receive a dunking, some quickly penciled facts and figures would be obliterated. Protecting our equipment from moisture for as long as possible was one of our most pressing cares. At last we were done. Slowly straightening our bent backs, we looked at each other and grinned. The final sorting was finished. While Ian and I finished stripping the bicycles and reorganizing the packing, John took three boxes of surplus gear back to Medellín by bus. He'd send them on to Panama by airfreight, after first mailing back to us at El Tigre all the jungle equipment which we'd packaged and left at Medellín.

For three days and nights Ian and I maintained a twenty-four-hour vigil for this most important cargo. Late on the third day it arrived. Ripping off string and fasteners, we stacked and packed each item into every conceivable pocket, corner, and hole of our packs. In anticipation of John's return, perhaps that very evening, we moved all our gear to the western side of the León River. After we crossed the small concrete bridge over this little river, all sign of the roadway vanished and a marked, slashed pathway greeted us.

We were now in the jungle we had wondered so long about. Trees and thick tropical growth towered over us, intertwining, seeking the sun's rays above. We stood flanked by waist-high grass, fallen and twisted stumps, mud holes, and majestic trees. The projected Pan-American Highway would one day force its tar-sealed way through nature's barriers—a gigantic undertaking. All I could see now of this highway was a road-wide strip of decaying jungle, felled by power saw and ax, that disappeared into the distance and marked the survey line—the beginning of "construction." We stood now on ground that gave under our weight, and the vegetation that brushed us was wet. This uneven, soft, brown, slimy ground would stay with us in the days ahead.

"Over here, Gary," Ian called, half hidden by broad leaves and roots. "We can store our stuff in here while we sling our hammocks," he suggested, freeing himself of his bulging, overweight backpack.

"Sounds good to me," I replied as I squatted to a position more suitable for removing my eighty-pound load.

Our first night in the jungle was an unusual experience. Nighttime was no longer quiet. Instead, animals rustled and jumped through leaves and low growth. Strange birds and insects filled the night air with unrecognizable sounds. John didn't arrive. It seemed hours before I finally fell into the realms of oblivion.

We had been using our hammocks since leaving Medellín, so sleeping in one now was as natural as sleeping in a bed. The night was stuffy and hot; sweat and itching became annoying. I was covered only by a light cotton blanket, more than enough at first, but toward dawn the tropical night grew chilly, and by morning I was rolled into a ball to stay warm.

The low mists and clearing skies heralded the beginning of another hot and humid swamp day. Our dislike of our staple breakfast of oatmeal grew more acute every morning. Ian and I shared the cooking duties that morning. As we began to clean the mess kit, suddenly a team of mules loaded with bags of rice and flour pushed through the green undergrowth. Close behind, mounted on a skinny, sweating horse, rode the man in charge of this supply team, relaxed, with a machete over his right shoulder. The team passed near us, sure-footed and calm over uncertain, rough terrain.

"Buenos dias, señor," came my hesitant Spanish.

"Bueno," he sighed, as his small horse maneuvered carefully, lifting its front hooves high to avoid hidden tree stumps.

He soon disappeared almost as quickly as he had come. Behind him, covered in glistening sweat and pushing forward along the same track, came John.

"Hi!" he greeted us. "Anything left to eat?"

"No, it's all finished. We're just about to move out and see what's ahead," I returned, putting away the last of the mess kit.

"You bring any fresh bread, John?" Ian added.

"Just a bit. It will have to do for my breakfast, I guess," he said, resting on the nearest safe branch he could find.

There had been no major hitch in Medellín. The equipment for Panama had been sent and was probably there already; our jungle equipment had arrived, and so had John. Everything was intact and not a single item had been stolen.

We brewed another cup of tea and shared these last few moments together before beginning. Keen, but excited, we talked, eager to begin our journey. We had all the aids we had been advised to bring along, and we were confident of our ability. But it was mid-March and the seasonal monsoons were now almost upon us. We were convinced that this surveyed line went directly west in a straight line to the Atrato River. But even though the distance to the river was only thirty-seven miles, it was through some of the most unhealthy and impassable swampland in the world, and this trail, sodden and half submerged, ended at the twenty-seven-mile peg.

What lay beyond that for the final ten miles was unknown. Our crude survey map showed a path still existing, but it told us nothing about its condition. Our present trail was passable only with extreme difficulty, but we would discover that what we were experiencing now was like a concrete footpath compared to what it would become.

▲▼▲

9

Our Lifeline Strained

Starting through the Atrato Swamp

Loaded down with a heavy pack and carrying his bike, John teetered precariously out along a shaking branch across an expanse of black, foul water. He carefully picked his way, steadying himself the best he could under the weight of his bike. The particular branch he chose arched upward to a massive fallen trunk. We had debated it before he began but figured this route was the quickest and safest. The other alternative was to wade through the stagnant slime that was belly and chest deep. Carefully John inched forward, gaining more height than distance, it seemed. Then he froze and swayed, trying to keep upright. I watched, my eyes glued to him as he swayed one way then the other—almost too far, but not quite. His face contorted with the effort. His boots didn't move; his chance of finding another foothold quickly enough on a branch this size was nearly impossible. If he lost his balance, he would plunge down into the putrid swamp water with the added risk of impaling himself on hidden splinters. I glanced down at the dead leaves floating on the black water.

John still clung to the small moss-covered branch hardly daring to breathe, eyes focused on the jungle ahead, body tense, muscles tight. The seconds slid by, then quietly he moved his weight nearer the larger end of the trunk. "Two more strides and he's there!" John plunged the final step and a half, then turned to look back at me standing knee deep in water, waiting my turn.

"Come, come, laddy," he said enticingly, grinning at me.

I followed, carefully placing one foot ahead of the other. To my relief, I made it. Together we moved over one obstacle after another but completed only half a mile before lunchtime.

Conditions deteriorated every step of the way, and I wondered just how long we would be in the Atrato. The huge jungle trees that had been cut, had fallen in every direction, creating a grotesque maze of splintered wood, brittle branches, and slippery trunks. Combined with an entanglement of dying vines and aquatic growth, it made walking so arduous that we were already becoming weak and tired. Yet, what we were experiencing now probably was not as bad as what lay ahead of us. Here, at least, we did have a debris-strewn track to follow.

During these first few days, we quickly worked our camping and packing routine into streamlined efficiency, but the effort of moving even a short distance down the trail was incredible. Both John and I became expert at climbing and balancing on branches while loaded with a heavy pack and carrying our bikes. Ian, who was doubtful of his ability to climb and balance, had to wade. Where John and I could climb on logs, Ian had to plow through chest-high water. His progress was appallingly slow; John and I could cover the same distance in half the time. But in this perilous terrain it would be folly to split up, so our speed was determined solely by the slowest member of the party. John and I were frustrated at being held back, but Ian suffered the mental strain of being the cause of our delay and his tension, in turn, affected us all since he frequently lost his self-control. In addition, we were all beginning to suffer from immersion foot, a condition which caused inflammation and stabbing pain.

Not only did we have to fight for every foot of mileage, but we had to fight against nature as well. We were attacked incessantly by mosquitoes, horseflies, and a million other biting or stinging insects. We also had come upon—often nearly stood upon—several small snakes and lizards. Slowly we became accustomed to our environment and learned to expect the unexpected and be ready to react to protect ourselves as quickly as God allowed us.

Our slow progress created another more serious problem—one that endangered the success of the whole project. It was taking us too long; our supplies were running low. Ten miles from the Atrato River and civilization, even this excuse for a trail would end abruptly, and we would be cutting our own path. We were already weak and tired. Although this survey line was chaos, it was at least a clear path with marker pegs to give us a precise idea of how far we had come. It was obvious that when we reached its end our forward momentum would be even further reduced, maybe as much as half. We needed a resupply of food if we were to reach the Atrato River and, eventually, dry land.

On the eighth day of swamp travel, much to our surprise we slogged into a clearing that had an Indian living in it. Weak from exhaustion and hunger, we stumbled toward it. In broken Spanish John asked the native man if we could buy some rice, sugar, and a few bananas. He shook his head; no, he would not share his supplies. He had only enough for his family. Conversation confirmed the information on our survey map: the marked path ended in about two more miles. Gloom descended. Maybe the man would take John in his boat to a small village on the Atrato River, Puerto Libre. If he refused to do this, we would have to abandon the remaining miles of swamp travel. Fortunately the man realized our necessity. John finally persuaded him to do the trip to Puerto Libre and back for the exorbitant fee of twenty dollars in American currency.

The next day, March 29, ten days from the road, John climbed into the dugout and headed toward the village of Puerto Libre to buy more oatmeal, rice, and any canned meat he could lay his hands on. This left Ian and me to ferry the gear to the end of the track and there to await John's return. The original track continued to be atrocious. We balanced on branches no bigger than three or four inches in diameter and waded through waist-high leaf mold and decaying trees. Rationing became an unpleasant reality. We carefully measured every cup of rice and oats so that if John were delayed we would still have a little to eat.

Our bodies cried out for nourishment, so at 11:30 we called a halt. Lighting a fire in the middle of the swamp is an art. The only dry place was on the roots of a dead tree. Ian and I carefully selected the least wet leaves and twigs, heaped them together, sprinkled a few drops of our valuable kerosene over them, and they were ready to ignite. With a small blue cloud of thick smoke, the leaves and brittle twigs burned—and died. "Try again or we don't eat," I told myself angrily. More carefully this time, I stacked a twig upon a leaf, and a leaf upon a twig, added a sprinkle of kerosene, then applied the match. The smoldering remains of the first attempt gave extra heat and a few

▲▼▲

agonizing moments later the small fire came to life. It could fall at any second from its precarious perch into the surrounding swamp water, but for the time being we had our fire. Once the rice was on and boiling, our next move was to rid ourselves of saturated shirts, trousers, and socks. Two hours soon passed while we ate our meager portions and talked, wondering how John was doing on his dugout ride.

The next two days saw no sign of John. Our food was almost exhausted. How long could we last?

Our food had consisted almost totally of oatmeal, rice, sugar, and soup which we carried in bulk up to ten pounds. When we were able, we purchased what we could—cheese, meat, jam—to supplement our diet. In the jungle few extras were ever available. Now even the very basic foodstuff was failing. I viewed my small, rationed portion of rice with new respect. It might be one of my last meals.

On April 1, 1972, Ian and I reached the end of the survey trail. Here the once sturdy heliport used for oil exploration was sunk unevenly in the soft bottom of the swamp, rotting beside twelve fifty-five-gallon diesel drums. It was a foreboding sight to behold. In front of us was all that was left of the path of a once moving project. What had happened?

That night as we served our last tin of oatmeal in cold aluminum plates, John stepped through the mud and slime to join us. Shouts of welcome sprang spontaneously from Ian and me. Now we could eat something besides oatmeal and rice.

We had not realized it, but there was at least one hornets' nest near the spot we were erecting our camp. At all this shouting they hurried out to defend their territory, and I was the victim. I left my half-slung hammock, running and stumbling over weeds and water, hotly pursued by a cloud of them. Several had firm holds on both my ears, while the rest gave their undivided attention to the back of my neck. Yelping in pain and flaying my arms madly about my head, I splashed through water and leaves, finally falling and resting in mud and ooze. My head and neck throbbed and soon became inflamed. The hornets, now completely satisfied with their defense, returned triumplantly to resume their previous activities. I slung my hammock elsewhere.

The final night on the trail we spent in wet hammocks. The rain fell incessantly from the dark heavens. It drowned out all other sounds and kept me awake as it dripped through flaking waterproofing and saturated the already damp canvas. It was cold and I shivered violently in the early morning hours. When dawn broke, even the driest areas of the previous night were now awash, and we had to take every step in cold water at least calf high. Chilled, wet vegetation grabbed at our goose-pimply limbs. Our little half-pint Primus stove flared into life to cook our monotonous breakfast of porridge.

Now compass and machetes would be used to the full. The track had ended. It was obvious that the monsoon rains were hard on our heels. Conditions certainly would not improve. No path of any description existed between our present position and the eastern bank of the Atrato River. With our food supply renewed, we had about twelve days' worth if we rationed ourselves. Had we been able to transport more, we would have done so, but physically speaking that was impossible. With packs pinning us deeper in the swamp mud, and bicycles to maneuver as well, we were all stretched to the limit of our capability.

Our projected track had remained seventy degrees west of north ever since we had started. Checking for a final time, we struck off into dense eight-foot-high swamp vegetation on this same bearing. After the rain of the night before, the entire area was under three or four more inches of water. What previously would have reached only up to my thighs, now completely saturated my hips. This soon caused irritation and bad chafing.

I tried hard to figure out just what staggering obstacles were still ahead. Thoughts tripped through the haze in my mind. "Roughly twelve miles to go before we reach the Atrato; a little over twelve days' food to our credit. Can we slash our way through stuff as thick as this in twelve long, hard days? How long can we last?"

Progress was unbelievably slow, crushing our morale. Where we had previously made a mile a day, we now worked hard to make a half mile. General fatigue, travel conditions, plus relentless attacks from ants took a devastating toll on our physical stamina and mental tolerance.

At times the pressure of circumstances brought thoughtless accusations and angry words that were almost overpowering. If we were to survive these hard days and to work together under extreme conditions, the words spoken in folly had to be ignored. Too much was at

▲▼▲

stake to risk anything so foolish. Toleration—of circumstances, food, and each other—became a paramount virtue. It took every last ounce of patience I had to bear these things, accept them, and remain silent in order not to contribute to the intensely delicate, explosive situation.

Our physical needs were not being met. We were undernourished; fatigued to the point of exhaustion; clad in foul, rotting clothing; and breaking out with immersion foot and boils. Our eyelids swelled and we were in increasing discomfort from internal parasites. Ian had been laboring increasingly since we had entered the swamp and now made no attempt to conceal the fact. My insides were very uneasy, and I no longer relished eating. A small portion of rice, soup, or oats would immediately activate the parasites in my stomach, and a deep feeling of gnawing numbness would envelop me. This sickened me and therefore gave me not an ounce of benefit for the energy I had expended. During the next days the terrain did not alter; we grew sicker daily. We were exhausted at lunch, and by dinner only able to climb slowly into our waiting hammocks before dark.

In our present situation, it was easy to see that our continuing survival depended on Someone greater than ourselves. Although we continued to suffer both physically and mentally, there were events that couldn't be explained rationally. These situations were first openly acknowledged by John, but I also felt that we were being looked after in a different kind of way.

One night I lay quietly in my hammock mulling over the hazards we had overcome. I drew a mental list of what might have happened: impaled on hidden splintered branches, arms and legs broken in a fall, drowning in some cesspool of muck, attacked by insects, fatal snake bites, or death by starvation. All these might-have-been events rumbled through my mind. None of these had happened, yet we had slipped many times on wet branches and occasionally had fallen heavily under loads. Ian had had one narrow escape from drowning when his pack pulled him down. I had seen many large snakes and so had John. We had been stuck in tight spots and had looked at one another with hungry, sick eyes; but somehow, we had always come through. We had even been able to find just the correct number of trees to sling three hammocks every night. Was this only luck?

The narrow path we were hacking was our lifeline back to civilization. It was now strained to its limit as we persistently cut our way westward. To my way of thinking, this much good luck could not be described as chance. John and I often talked about life at the lunch breaks and while we prepared the evening's rice. He was sure that Huey, as he called God at that time, was looking after us. I wasn't yet sure this was completely correct. But I had to admit that I believed in God. Was He interested in our welfare in a place like this? The weeks and months to follow were to convince me even further of the love and sovereignty of God. A new awakening was coming—not physical or mental awareness—but, rather, a completely new spiritual dimension. God in His own way and time would impress upon me that the weaker we became, the more His love and provision for us abounded.

Deep inside I knew the reality of physical torture, mental anxiety, and spiritual emptiness. The months ahead continued to try our mental processes as well as our physical endurance.

After a 35 day ordeal, Gary arrives at the first Indian village outside the Atrato Swamp.

▲▼▲

10

Webbed Feet Forever?

Leaving the Atrato

Teetering on half a dozen large, soft stems of undergrowth, I was sinking rapidly. Ahead somewhere I could hear John crashing through and hacking at the undergrowth. With my last strength I heaved the bike forward and sent it crashing headlong into the quagmire. The energy that propelled the bike forward only succeeded in burying me deeper in thick slime and water. Two strides in front of me lay a large bottomless hole with my bike now on its far side. I could still hear John up ahead. Using as much cut growth as I could, I began making footrests along the side of the cesspool. Every movement sucked me down further into the bog.

"If a man had webbed feet, he just wouldn't be in a position like this!" I said to myself. My ears listened for the chopping. It had stopped. "John must be taking a break," I hoped. "Or is he in a situation like me—up to his armpits?"

My right foot rested lightly on my flimsy footrest, but the weight of my body with my backpack held me in the clutches of the mire. It took enormous force to push my bulk forward out of that position. Finally I lay sprawled alongside the hole. Covered in sweat, grime, and mud, I listened intently for noise up ahead. I heard nothing. Grabbing my waterlogged bike and pulling myself to my feet, I struggled along through thigh-deep water. To my surprise, the track took a sharp left turn and seemed to almost disappear.

"John-o must have run into another hornets' nest," I grinned. "He changed direction kinda sudden-like."

It was not uncommon for the cutter to blindly steer his back into a large ants' or hornets' nest while he concentrated on the compass bearing and his slashing. The resulting spontaneous reaction propelled him

111

forward with a remarkable speed and agility that he didn't otherwise possess. It was bad news at the time, but something to laugh about later on in the day.

I continued to stumble along a meandering track, still straining for further sound up ahead, stopping every few paces in an effort to catch the slightest movement or call. Again the track veered sharply, and as I rounded the bend I saw John waist high in water at the base of a medium-sized, spiky tree. He was motionless, trying to summon the energy to climb the root system and eventually the tree. He turned in my direction as I waded closer.

"Welcome. If I can remove myself from here, I'm going to play I-spy with the Atrato River," he cracked.

"Suits me. We've gotta be close. Even the map indicates that!" I replied.

With a few grunts and groans John extracted himself from the muck and stood at the tree's base, dripping and cold. Up he went, over spikes and foliage, gripping with hands and boots as best he could.

"Well, well, well! Guess what I see?" he shouted.

"The river! Is it the river?" I yelled.

"Two or maybe three huts, laddy. They're pretty close," he enthused.

"Check your compass bearing, John. Are they on our course or not?"

"No, they're not. But if we change to forty degrees west of north, we'll hit'em. I'd say about half a mile off, maybe a little more," he estimated.

"We've nearly made it, John-o. We've nearly made it!"

"There's also a small outcrop of palms just over to the right of us. Good for hammocks if we can make it by nightfall," he added.

Suddenly we heard a cry of desperation. John and I froze, looking at each other, mortified and unbelieving.

"That's Ian!"

The sudden chilling yell sent shivers up my spine. I dropped my bike and backpack and began struggling along the track toward the sound. Ian could be caught and weighted down or have been attacked by something or caught off guard, falling out of his depth.

My lungs heaved and my legs clung heavily to the swamp as my pace decreased to a labored stumble. I could not force the energy into

▲▼▲

my tired and strained body any longer.

Then I caught sight of him. Ian had fallen into the hole I had just managed to circumvent; now he struggled wildly for a foothold or handgrip. Somehow his floundering hands and feet found enough leverage to thrust him clear. Slowly Ian picked up his once brilliant blue bicycle and wheeled it past me to the track's end. Without resting for a second, he went back to get his pack and bring it up to the tree. I could see from his white face and drawn expression that he, most of all, needed to be rid of this bitter existence. Being older than either John or I, the physical drain on him had been substantially greater, so he suffered far more distress.

Our backpacks were now significantly lighter, as today was our twenty-fourth in the swamp; our rations consisted of a single two-pound can of oatmeal. The big question was whether we would be able to reach the Atrato River before starving.

I carried on, hacking soft growth and holding the compass needle at forty degrees west of north in a last effort to reach those palms by nightfall. Rain fell heavily as I labored on, knee, thigh, and at times, chest deep in water. After this monsoon storm, the water level would rise dramatically. Exhausted, my left arm bleeding and swollen from continued exposure to sharp vegetation, I drove my machete into the first palm and whispered to myself in relief, "Made it!"

Shortly afterward I heard John splash up from behind, grunting and heaving, trying desperately not to lose his temper. The bases of several of the trees enabled us to stand above the watery ground. Instinctively we searched for the highest mound and surveyed the tree trunk.

"You're the expert, John-o. Up you go!"

He didn't need more prompting; within thirty seconds he was over halfway up the tree, as high as he needed to be.

"I can see the river! Oh you beautiful, beautiful baby!" he shouted and laughed down to me.

"I don't believe you," came my stunned response. "Where are those three huts you saw?"

"On the other side of the river, Gary. They're on the other side! We're only a couple hundred yards from the eastern bank of the Atrato River! Tomorrow we get out!"

We were both jubilant and full of self-congratulation. John climbed down, and we shook each other by the hand, laughing and smiling, forgetting for a time just how awful we felt.

John had had his bike and pack with him when he'd caught up with me, so he started the fire while I returned to keep Ian company and pick up my own gear. The evening meal was a ration apiece of uncooked oatmeal, using the last of our powdered milk and white sugar. We had traversed the great Atrato Swamp, a distance of thirty-seven miles, and had survived with a can of oatmeal left over!

We slept restlessly even though we were dog tired. Tonight was our final night sleeping over water; tomorrow would see us on dry land—speaking to Colombians, eating bread and meat, and drinking soft drinks.

The next day—Friday, April 14, 1972—John, Ian, and I, together with three bicycles, three hammocks, three packs, and not much else, finally stood on the far bank of the Atrato—fourteen days from the end of the survey trail, and after a total of twenty-six days of swamp survival. We had attracted the Indians' attention, and in a rush they transported us from the swamp's edge to their village. We stayed there one night before moving on to Sautatá, a cattle ranch several miles downriver opposite the town of Puerto Libre. Here, we were told, the owner spoke English and would probably allow us to recover for a week or two.

Unknown to us, the British Range Rover Expedition, traveling from Panama to Colombia via the Darién Gap, now had their base situated on the Sautatá airstrip and were busy finding alternate routes around the swamp we had just crossed. They welcomed us with open arms, and we spent long hours together discussing the route they had followed through the Darién Jungle.

They had information on villages and conditions about which we knew nothing, and over our first meal of meat and greens in a month, they shared what they knew. In our lengthy and detailed conversations, I was to see that God had again provided for a change in our plans. We had previously planned to cross the Darién via the mountainous San Blas region to avoid any possibility of a floodwater holdup. Tracks through this northern area did exist as far as Acandi on the Panamanian border, but after that we weren't sure whether there were any or not. Over a freshly cooked meal of beef, eggs, french fries, and cabbage, the three of us discussed our options at length. Several

▲▼▲

important points influenced our decision to abort our plan to follow the northern route and to reroute ourselves along the same trails that had been used by the British expedition. First, the monsoon season had already broken, and storms similar to the ones we had experienced in the swamp would become more frequent. Second, it would be foolish to ignore such sound advice and detailed information concerning the entire route into the city of Panama. If we were not delayed, this should prove a faster route, and we might yet beat the main rains that would shortly inundate the country. Third, they could pinpoint for us small villages that were closer together and outnumbered those we'd find by going along the Caribbean coast. At these villages we should be able to purchase food, making our supply line more secure. These points carried a lot of weight, but the sealing factor was that just over the Panamanian border, approximately thirty miles from Sautatá, where we were, was the small Cuna Indian village of Paya. A missionary couple ministering to the Indians and studying their language lived there. From them we could probably get medical treatment for our severe intestinal parasites, immersion foot, and festering boils.

The die cast, all that remained was a drying-out period and good food. Unhygienic conditions, including nothing but swamp water to drink, had completely derailed our normal digestion. Before entering the swamp, we could easily eat a full-sized meal; now a meal a fourth that size uncomfortably filled our stomachs. Although we ate continuously the first week we were at Sautatá, our bodies didn't benefit at all. Any nourishment we took merely fed the already thriving worms that continued to sap our strength. Something was drastically wrong with our systems, and the only chance of qualified treatment lay at Paya.

During the second and final week of our layoff, our itchy immersion-foot complaints and slashed forearms did completely heal, however. And the large crop of septic boils Ian had nursed on the small of his back in the latter days of swamp travel responded to harsh treatment by the head stockman. We were at least outwardly well, we three crazy men who had tackled the Atrato—and won!

▲▼▲

11

Jungle-style Hospital

In the Darién Jungle

Slippery mud on steep trails made progress slow and gut-wrenching. As we labored through the Darién Jungle, John and I were again heavily ladened with bulging backpacks of food purchased at Sautatá. Ian, up ahead, carried all he could manage and still remain on his feet for a day.

Jungle had once shrouded the damp track in darkness, but now, thanks to the work of the Range Rover expedition, tiny shafts of sunlight penetrated through. In the gray stillness of the protective undergrowth, insects, moths, and ants diligently went about the task of survival. How much at home they seemed! Watching them reminded me how far out of our accustomed environment we were. The snapping and crackling of foliage never ended, causing me to often flinch, stop, and turn quickly to identify its source. With a rustle of dead foliage, a lizard would flash into sight, caught unawares. I would stop, looking directly into dark, piercing, cold eyes. They would return my stare, seeming to bore through me. The flecks of green and black camouflaged them beautifully. Had I missed the panicked flights, I couldn't have spotted them in that leafy carpet. Their color blend was perfect.

Such experiences caused me to think more closely about the infinite wisdom of God who was said to have created all this. Man, I thought, He sure did a great job on that lizard's coloring. I looked down at my feet. Not six inches away lay an unused and long forgotten ant trail. We had seen many such trails before, bristling with activity. "Who programmed them?" I wondered.

▲▼▲

John came heaving up from behind me, rested his bike against a stump, and dropped his rotting pack full of rice and oatmeal.

"What's the matter, laddy? Gut troubling you again?" He was right, but I tried to avoid the question by pointing out the habits of the ants.

"What makes `em tick, John-o? It's instinct, isn't it? Just like a cow when she's dropped her calf. Why does she turn around and lick at its head? Instinct, nothing else."

"Well," John replied as he eased himself down onto a fallen log, "I guess you're right. Take a sheep, for instance. She does the same thing after giving birth. And what about a turtle? Now there's instinct for you, returning to the same place each year to lay eggs."

"Yeah," I answered. "And when you consider the earth and all the forces involved, the whole concept is incredible, isn't it? But my question is this: who put the instinct there? And who put the earth together and all the laws that govern life? Man doesn't create the laws of gravity or light, for instance; they were in existence. We just happened to discover them, right?"

"Guess you're right, Gary," agreed John. "There has to be a God. Obviously no one in his right mind would deny the evidence of that. But, so what? So He has given us all this. Great! But is that where it all ends?"

I was starting to shrug back into my pack when John suddenly leaped from his jungle armchair.

"Oh no you don't!" he sneered at a platoon of inch-long black ants ready to attack. Out from its sheath came his machete, and with several venomous slaps with the breadth of his blade, he crushed his would-be assailants. Black ants had stung John in the early days of swamp travel, injecting a poisonous serum. It had taken several days for his glands to return to normal, leaving him sore and watchful for their next attack. He didn't intend for that to occur again here in the Darién.

My stomach and intestines gave a hollow growl. The empty feeling inside was becoming worse, and each step toward the Panamanian border was a struggle. "How's the gut?" I asked. I was anxious to know whether he was suffering as violently as I.

"Bad. And I'm not kidding," he answered, looking straight into my eyes, serious, not a smile on his haggard face.

▲▼▲

I noticed how the points of his once heavily muscled shoulders now stood out. His pale flesh and puffy eyes showed his exhaustion and pain. He had been a rock of stability and had spurred on my flagging spirits. I had done the same for him, giving a word of encouragement or a quiet comment when his blood ran hot. Our pace was incredibly slow because our health was breaking up, even after a two-week layoff on the best food we had had in months. John's saturated hat sat atop his soaked curly hair; his clothes clung wet and rotting to his ailing frame. With his machete slung on his left side, and boots that were falling away from his feet, he stood bedraggled, tired, and every inch my companion—a man I could trust with my life.

A tremendous bond of friendship had been forged in the early days of the swamp trek, and here in the jungle it came out stronger than ever. Under these stressful conditions we had discovered one another's strengths and weaknesses, and we had learned to see beneath each other's bad points to the underlying character.

It was a common goal and a common enemy that kept our three-man comradeship tolerable. At times, circumstances, combined with almost unbearable internal suffering, distorted situations out of proportion. Everyday matters assumed paramount importance in minds distraught by the need for a change of pace, a change of diet, and a return to civilization. There had been times in the past, and assuredly would be ahead, when the struggle just to climb the next slippery bank took more than we had to give. As it was, the perpetually soaked clothing and gear cut and chafed, rubbing large red raw areas between our legs. We had to be constantly on the alert for attacks by ants, mosquitoes, snakes, scorpions, or spiders. We sweated and strained for every inch of ground we gained, and we fought the stench of our sweat and grime and the urge to scratch, which would just worsen the pock-marked raw areas. In the midst of all this discomfort, we wondered how we could remain united, a party of three men. How could we still keep our purpose to traverse the Darién and willingly expose ourselves to more of the torture under which we existed?

On John's face I read things that he could never have expressed— feelings that made him cry silently, inwardly, feelings that in a few months could be fully expressed. But not now. Now, both of us knew our strength didn't lie in ourselves, since we had nothing worth giving anymore. (Nothing that would make a difference, anyway.) We would

▲▼▲

have to take each day as it came, play it by ear, and be ready to react to the unexpected behind the next log, around the next corner, or in the next overhanging tree. We were constantly on guard.

Ian remained ahead, as we had previously arranged. We lightened his load as much as possible, for now to our consternation, his right ankle had broken out. The joint and lower shin were badly swollen and covered with infection. Mucus from the sores dried and crusted to the reddened extremity.

Ian had only just recovered at Sautatá from five septic boils on his back. He faced the same uncertainties as John and I, as well as others. Ian's leg swelled badly and throbbed incessantly after each day's travel, making it impossible to go any faster. White, pale, and drawn, a man fighting nature with reserves he didn't know he possessed, Ian eked out of each day the distance God afforded him. He was striving beyond all his physical and mental limits with the same frustrations and illness as I. But, in addition, he was torn by the knowledge that he was slowing progress for us all and the desperate determination to reach Paya before his rotting right ankle completely immobilized him.

My concern grew when I overtook him one day leaning limply against a nearby tree. His shoulders were slumped forward, his head low, his mouth open, gasping, and he was unable to speak. I wondered how much more he could take and still press forward.

"Border's just up ahead," I encouraged. Ian was past replying, but it annoyed me when he gave no response. He shivered as he stooped to sling his pack, then leaned painfully into his bike and struggled up the remaining slope to the summit. Stagger, slip, and slide, he started his ascent, paused, then repeated the same motions. From the base of that last climb, I watched a sick and weakened man, once strong and sure, cross over into Panama amid the cold rolling clouds of mist.

Indians who had passed us on the trail several days before sat nearby as we finished our usual helping of rice and soup for lunch. A Chocó Indian family, traveling to the same village we were, became friendly enough to venture nearer. The elderly man, clad only in a red loincloth, held out two large, salted fish for us to enjoy. His stained teeth punctuated a large, broad smile. It was a kind and unusual offer from an Indian who could sense the illness and strangeness we felt. The natural nakedness of the women blended into their surroundings and was to be expected in the region we were passing through. They chattered and laughed among themselves as we sampled the fish. The feeling of white meat lining our stomachs was a welcome change from being filled with rice, although it was so heavily salted that it burned our throats, made our eyes water, and forced us to reach for the water canteen.

A cold, crumbling concrete slab marked the border between Colombia and Panama. Signs of the Range Rover campsite still remained. Bottles, papers, cans, and rain shelters were scattered within a small radius of the cleared central area; the track skirted around it before quietly slipping into the foliage already struggling to engulf it.

We figured Paya to be, at most, about one and a half days away. We were close to medical help and English-speaking missionaries! How comforting that became. It superceded and even seemed to overcome the spasms of diarrhea and nauseating dizziness.

Chilled air now caught us as we lay in the dampness of the morning. White clouds hung onto the tops of the towering timber. Rolling and billowing, they floated high above, reaching down to ground level momentarily, then leaping upward again. Soaked moss and fungus grew profusely on tree trunks, saturating us if we carelessly brushed past too close.

As we descended from the moist clouds, the familiar signs of habitation and cultivation appeared again, and then we heard the roar of the long-sought tributary. Soon we were viewing, then crossing, the Paya River. In the distance, pressed in by jungle, lay the first small, thatch-roofed hut. Exhausted, we followed the muddy jungle path toward what we hoped was the main village. A stream of small Cuna Indian boys tagged after us as we shuffled into Paya, seeking the gringo missionary the British expedition had told us about.

Keith Forster stood tall, solid, white, and somehow out of place in this village. His wife, Wilma, a Canadian, greeted us with a smile and looked at us with concern. A trained nurse, she easily read the signs of jungle sicknesses.

"Glad to see you guys are safe," Keith remarked in his South African-accented English. "I had heard by bush telegraph that you'd made the border. I began wondering after you didn't show in two days. It's normally only an eight-hour walk."

"Well, we've had a few problems, and it rained cats and dogs up there," Ian replied. "It took a bit longer than we expected." (In fact, it

▲▼▲

had taken us three days to cover the distance!)

John cut in hurriedly, "Is there any chance of buying meat in the village, Keith? And maybe some fresh eggs?"

"We'll see what we can round up," Keith comforted, his reply assuring us that we would at least be able to purchase a small chicken.

Within an hour, we had bought one chicken, several bunches of bananas, and a few precious eggs. The village itself was short on food, and I wondered why people lived like this when river transportation was available to replenish supplies.

All that first day we kept our sicknesses to ourselves, not wanting to bother either of them for treatment since they were packing to leave by plane for Panama City. Their small, thatched, dirt-floor hut was a hive of activity as they sorted boxes of equipment and shelves of medicines.

Keith could see the loneliness on our faces and hear desperation in our questions about what lay ahead. Over meals and at evening discussions we shared the swamp experiences with them and told them about what we were struggling to accomplish. They listened, engrossed in our tales, not believing that men had survived such a crossing. Finally, we told them, after many hours of conversation, just how unwell and infected we had become. Feeling that someone cared for us, we gave Wilma graphic descriptions of our symptoms.

Ian remained strangely silent about his ankle. He was drawn and tired, thankful for this haven and for the three or four days he could stay off his leg. One night Wilma distributed several packs of pills designed to rid our intestines of worms. With her instructions on dosages clear in our minds, we left their small hut and walked by flashlight to where we had slung our hammocks. Keith had obtained permission from the young chief for us to sleep for four days in the large, newly constructed meeting house. At the end of those four days Keith and Wilma would fly out, leaving us to push on to the next village, Capetí.

The thought that these kind missionaries were supposed to have left Paya a month before we walked in staggered my mind. Why had they stayed? Was this another way that God was showing me how He provided? And why were Keith and Wilma so concerned for our health? Why was Wilma qualified to minister to our needs? How easily this little hut could have been empty when we arrived. God was

122

showing not only me, but all of us, something of His love for us. Here again, assistance and companionship had been put right in our path; yet, though I would accept the provision, I would not acknowledge in my own heart, much less to anyone else, that it was from God.

Each mealtime we shared the Forsters' canned food and wonderful, different friendship. These people were doing a marvelous job, ministering God's Word and assisting the Cuna people in every way they could.

Through their radio link to Panama, Keith was able to ask the Wycliffe office whether it would be possible for them to fly out our three-month accumulation of mail that was waiting at the British Embassy. We held onto our hopes as we impatiently sat out the pause between radio signals.

"We have been able to pick up mail for the cyclists. Man, they've got a heap!" a woman's voice said from the black set. John and I looked at each other, shouted, threw our arms up, laughed, and shook each other by the hand. News from home would find its way into the Darién Jungle via the Wycliffe Bible Translators' airplane. It was something we'd never hoped for or even dreamed about. Tomorrow maybe we could read it.

Ian was now literally hobbling on his sore leg. Immersion foot, coupled with the septic ankle infection, drastically impaired his walk. In a heated, unfeeling session, John and I both lost our tempers and told Ian to go show it to Wilma. Reluctantly he did. The leg smelled of decaying flesh. It was open and swollen. No words were necessary; all of us knew it was bad and needed immediate treatment if we were ever to walk to Panama City. The wound was washed, cleaned, and swabbed. Ian was put on a course of penicillin pills and told to rest.

On the next radio call we were told that bad weather had rained out the flight; the pilot would try tomorrow. We were disappointed, selfishly and unreasonably so, not wanting to accept the fact. That hot jungle night on May 13, 1972, we twiddled dials on Keith's transistor radio and, to our utter astonishment, picked up New Zealand—a mushy reception of the Mothers' Day request session. Our ears pricked up. We hung onto every word. Place names seemed sweeter than they had ever been before. The way the announcer spoke almost brought tears to my eyes. John and I sat there, oblivious to anything but the radio program. Mentally we were in New Zealand, 10,000 miles away

Choco Indian roundhouses were a familiar sight in the jungle area near the border of Colombia and Panama.

▲▼▲

and far from reality. With a crackle it faded into incomprehensible static.

That evening Keith and Wilma, though still in the midst of endless preparations for their departure, told us about the organization they represented and of their mission. It was because of a definite heartfelt call from God that they were here in Paya with the Cuna Indians. It was not by chance, nor choice, but the preference of God Himself. I admired what this couple were endeavoring to achieve here, but I could not see myself in a similar situation.

Keith ended the intense discussion of their beliefs and experiences by reading a small portion of the Bible. He invited our comments, but I could not venture any constructive view because I neither wanted nor cared for what God had done for me. "What has He done, anyway?" I asked myself. "The important thing is Ian's leg. If it doesn't respond to treatment, how can we move out? Bible reading may be OK, but I'm not so sure how practical it is. There are too many unknowns right now for me to concentrate on God at a time like this! Maybe when we get out of this bind I'll be able to think a little more deeply. The problems are here and now. I can't agree or figure out what to believe when our lives are so cluttered with details of our continued survival."

Something within me put up defenses, obstacles, traps, and excuses. The desire to avoid involvement was strong. I respected both Keith and Wilma for the lives that they led and for what they believed. But, this was not for me. We faced a further seven weeks' struggle and possible death. God was not what I needed now! John had been aggressive toward the Bible and was enraged by the number of hypocrites calling themselves Christians. Ian had once studied and become part of the Christian establishment, but whether or not he was a real Christian I did not know.

Silence enveloped the group while Keith gave us time to think of questions. None came; so shortly he closed with a word of prayer.

That night, before drifting into sleep, I pondered what had been said. I could call it coincidence and rationalize and explain as much as I wished, but there was still something about Keith and Wilma that gave them strength.

Ian's leg was not improved the next morning. It began to smell more, almost by the hour, and it was obvious that something else was needed. Wilma radioed back to Panama City to ask for a doctor's

125

advice. A qualified American doctor, a member of their church, gave instructions to continue swabbing the leg with boiling water and to give two injections of penicillin a day. The pills Ian had been taking had not been effective since his entire body was exhausted and needed to be replenished. His infection needed direct help which it would receive from a large dosage of penicillin both night and morning.

On Wednesday, May 17, the small airplane from Panama City approached the soggy landing strip, which was barely long enough for it to land. With a roar and sputter accompanied by flying mud and debris, Vic Hess brought his plane to a halt. Our hands extended warm greetings and eagerly received the long-awaited mail from home.

I learned from my own stack of blue aerograms that I had become an uncle for the second time. What really surprised me was that my brother and his wife had chosen to name their new son after me! It was great to know everyone was well and that life had been progressing normally in the last three months.

Keith and Wilma had given us invaluable assistance, but the next day they would fly with Vic Hess to Panama City, leaving us on our own. That last night Wilma asked whether John or I would be responsible for giving Ian his penicillin injections. We looked at one another, eyes asking and searching. After a few seconds of silence, John said, "Gary, you've had experience injecting animals. I haven't."

"True," I said, trying to visualize the implications. "OK. If we're ever going to get out of here, I guess it's my job. Show me what to do."

Expertly Wilma prepared the syringe, drugs, and alcohol. I watched closely while she emphasized cleanliness and proper procedure. In a moment or two the medicine was ready to administer. Ian was white in the darkness, back hunched, shoulder stiffly braced.

"Relax, Ian," I urged as I drove a two-and-a-half-inch needle into the flesh of his right arm. He caught his breath and turned away as I pushed the penicillin into his bloodstream. In a second it was over, his arm cleaned, and the syringe disposed of. One dose down with eight to go. Ian sat nursing his arm in obvious discomfort, dissatisfied with the entire situation.

The next morning, moments before they were due to fly, Wilma tugged at my shirt and beckoned me outside. She needed to explain the possible side effect of such a heavy dose of penicillin. "Ian is in very, very low physical condition," she explained, "and the injections

▲▼▲

could have an adverse effect even though they are necessary to heal him."

What is she saying? I wondered, expecting her to mention nothing more serious than a bruised arm.

"In his present state of health, Gary," she continued, "Ian is likely to go into shock. If that happens, this is what you'll have to do." She handed me two vials of manufactured adrenaline.

Slowly she went over the dosages with me, as well as the time intervals between the injections. I accepted the danger and the staggering responsibility that was now mine. Should Ian go into shock, I knew what I had to do to save his life. The medicine might lie between Ian and death.

The three of us watched our missionary friends lift high into the sky and disappear from view. Later that same afternoon I shared with John what Wilma had told me. At least he could help me bear the knowledge and watch Ian.

"You're carrying the medical kit, John. Wrap up the vials of penicillin and keep the adrenaline separate and hidden. I don't want Ian to know."

"Fine. Have we a spare syringe to keep with the adrenaline?" queried John.

"Yes, I think so. But whatever you do, John-o, keep it handy, and be sure to watch Ian closely. If anything strange happens, let me know quickly, OK?"

I was dead serious. From that day until I was satisfied there was no further danger of shock, Ian was to be watched every waking moment. John understood as well as I that should things go wrong Ian's life was at stake. This was too high a price to pay even for an overland record.

With these thoughts still in my head I sorted and packed my gear, getting it ready for our walk to Capetí. We had arranged with the Cuna Indians of Paya for a young man to guide us there.

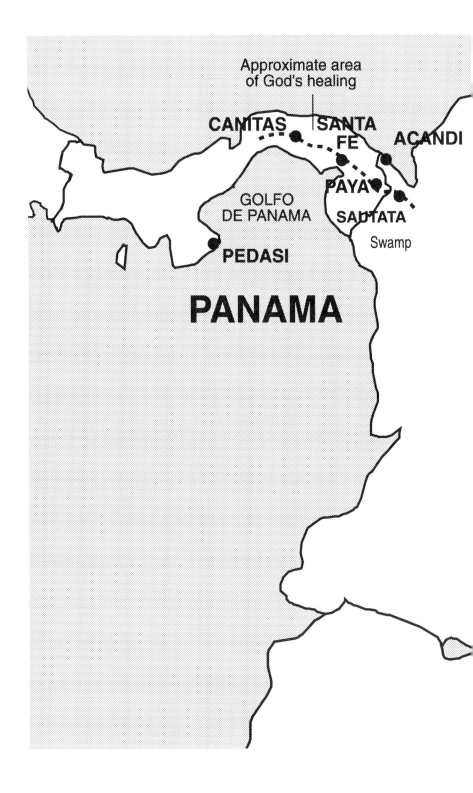

▲▼▲

12

Rested and Anxious to Move

In the Darién, from Paya to Santa Fé

We heard pounding on the ground for yards before John and I sloshed up behind our guide and Ian.

"What's the matter?" I asked, and then caught my breath as I saw the frantic actions of our guide.

With a piece of wood about four feet long, he was battering the life from a black and brown checkered snake. His face was set as he brought his mallet down hard on its oval-shaped head. Flesh from the snake splattered the immediate area, and blood clung to the wooden mallet. He paused, breathed, then dealt one more shattering blow, completely pulverizing the creature's head. He neither grinned nor smiled as he looked up, satisfied that the reptile was dead. He indicated snake fangs with the first two fingers of his hand; then with a sudden movement, he jerked his hand downward, conveying the idea of snakebite. Finally he shook his finger sideways to impress on us that this variety of snake was exceptionally dangerous.

"How close did you come to it?" asked John.

"I nearly stepped on it; it was right out on the path. I didn't even see the thing," came Ian's relieved reply.

John gave a low whistle and slowly shook his head. He took off his pack and laid his bike down in the mud. "Yours must be a charmed existence, Ian."

"Well, there's not much of the blighter left now," returned Ian as he rested on a rock near the watercourse.

"How's time, laddy?" John ventured.

"Twelve o'clock, I guess. Anyway, I reckon after all the excite-

■▼▲

ment, we can use more rice and soup, right?"

"That's just what we need." John unwrapped the blackened Primus stove. "Rice and soup."

Our diet, which had been supplemented during our break at Paya, now reverted to the monotony of rice, oatmeal, and soup.

"Let's get the water boiled for Ian's leg first," continued John.

"Sit down and take things easy, Ian," I urged. "Here, mix the soup while we boil the water."

Ian reclined heavily against his pack, removed his rotting boot, and rolled up his mud-laden trouser leg. I gathered the water, and within ten minutes it was ready for swabbing the infected area.

John reached in the medical kit for the bandage supplies Wilma had given us. I could see the strain on Ian's face as he applied the sterilized, hot water to his wound.

John manned the stove and started heating the rice. I needed to return to the stream for more water, but before doing so I whispered to John to keep an eye on Ian. He nodded his head, and I knew that I never really had to remind him.

I found a still area in the small trickle of jungle water, scooped out a pint, and relaxed on a rock. My stomach stirred, and my bowels felt weak. Those pills Wilma gave us sure are doing their job, I thought, and then charged into the undergrowth to relieve myself.

Weak and shaking, I returned up the slight rise to rejoin John and Ian. Our guide sat patiently watching all we did. He laughed at the jokes he understood and hurriedly ate his portion of the meal.

This young man of nineteen was the Paya chief's cousin. He was receiving three dollars a day for guiding us and carrying Ian's pack to Capetí. We anticipated a journey of two days plus one day for the guide's return. The agreement was that he would eat and sleep as we did and carry Ian's pack; we would pay him for his return trip to the village. The double job of guide and porter was a necessary part of the agreement. Ian was not able to keep up the pace with his sore leg. He was having trouble just handling his bike. If either John or I had been weighted down much more it would have been the straw that broke the camel's back; so this young Cuna played an important part in furthering our progress. It was expensive, but what other alternative did we have?

Gathering our gear from among the leaves, wood, dead branches, scorpions, and ants, we pushed forward through more mud. The foul-smelling ooze, stirred thick by rain, clung stubbornly to our boots and pants, cycle tires, and frames. Boots took on new characteristics; they were twice their normal size and more than three times their original weight. Every stride required increased effort—more pull to extract each foot in turn, more to lift it forward, more energy to slam it back into the mire from which it had come. Leg muscles stretched and flexed, crying out for relief—relief that was not possible, relief that would only come once they had carried us another 200-odd miles.

The second day from Paya we found the upper reaches of the Capetí River and camped by the foaming flow. In two days we had not found the village nor seen any people or habitations. Tomorrow we would be without our guide because, as we had previously arranged, he would return home.

Around our small campfire, situated several feet above the Capetí headwaters, we sat exhausted, cooking our food. All of us washed except Ian, who continued swabbing his right ankle. Dusk descended swiftly under the blanket of drooping growth as I prepared the penicillin injection for him.

"You ready for your shot?" I asked, pumping any air out of the syringe.

"Yep," came his tight-lipped reply as he rolled up his sleeve. He stiffened as I pinched his muscle and drove in the sterile needle. Even after I withdrew it and had dabbed his arm with alcohol, Ian continued to grip his shoulder and pace back and forth along the slippery mud trail. My eyes never left him. I watched his face contort in discomfort, then relax only to grimace again. These shots made him feel sick and uncomfortable, but if he didn't receive two a day, his leg would continue to decay.

John carried on with his cooking tasks, frequently looking at Ian to observe the effect of the penicillin. In fifteen minutes Ian's reaction steadied and he visibly relaxed. The worst was over for this time and I continued with the job of swinging my hammock on two substantial Panamanian trees.

The next morning, our third from Paya, we awoke to a beautiful sunrise. We had asked our guide to remain with us as long as possible on that last day. This he did, leaving us, once we recrossed the river, with directions to follow this water until we reached Capetí. We were grateful for his assistance and paid him in crisp dollar bills. He beamed, shook our hands, recrossed the river, then quickly disappeared behind thick, tight, vegetation. Now we were on our own, at least until we arrived at the village.

That afternoon found us dazed and tired, wandering over impossible tracks, stumbling into fallen logs and dead-end blinds, and dropping into animal trails. After fruitless searching and pawing over leads and insignificant suggestions of leads, we had to admit to ourselves that our trail had disappeared. Signs of life had diminished, telltale imprints had become more and more scarce as we advanced into tangled and matted undergrowth. While I stood pondering the placement of my next step, I heard the barking and rustling of an animal. Head cocked, knees braced, I held my machete ready. John had heard the distant sound also and turned around to catch it more fully.

"Is that a dog?" Ian asked.

"Sounds like it. That means we're not that far off the track," I reasoned.

Soon came the sound of feet on earth, heavy breathing, and an occasional shout.

"Directly behind, Gary," Ian stated, sagging under his pack.

"Right. Must be a hunting party," I replied.

John gazed back along the ragged track over which we had just hauled our bikes.

The sound of approaching life grew nearer and nearer, drumming the ground, stirring the undergrowth.

Suddenly, out of the entangled growth came the first Chocó Indian. He stopped, dogs beside him, rifle in hand, staring almost unbelieving. His fellow tribesmen soon crowded behind him, looking over his shoulder with interest at what blocked their path home. They had freshly slaughtered animals roped to their backs and were clad in the familiar loincloth. Hesitatingly they asked where we were going.

"Capetí," John stated firmly, and in his best Spanish asked for directions. Indeed they did know the whereabouts of the village. In fact, these five Chocó Indians were from that very camp and were hurrying back home before darkness caught them.

I glanced at my watch—2:00 P.M. They told us that their village was almost four hours' walk away. We had to remember that that was the time they could walk it in. The time for three crazy gringos with packs and bicycles was another question. The Indians agreed to help Ian carry his pack and bicycle after we explained that he had a bad leg and would be unable to move so quickly.

Eight men now heaved and ran along the track, over riverbeds and up sheer banks, teetered in footholds cut in trunks and hauled, lugged, and stretched over cut timbers. Indian helped white man, stranger became friend, guide became helper—truly another godsend. Our communication was severely limited by language barriers, but these five Chocó hunters knew where we had to go and knew how to get us there the best and quickest way.

The shadows grew long as the tropical sun sank lower into a green curtain, giving diffused lighting to a darkening scene. I glanced at my watch again. "Good grief, it's nearly 5:30 P.M.," I told myself. "No wonder it's getting dark. Man, this place had better turn up mighty soon."

Our twisting track continued to dip and rise, cross water beds, climb banks, and cross fallen timbers. "How on earth could we have followed it through conditions like these?" I questioned as we slid down the slippery bank.

With the final light of the day, we staggered into Capetí, bedraggled, sweating, and thankful that we had found our way. Was it coincidence or good luck? It was a provision from God in an extremely delicate situation.

Ian brought up the rear. Feeling the effects of his leg, he sat heavily on the nearest thing he could find.

Naked children and women viewed us from their round houses, curious about our next move. We had just stripped off our boots, shirts, and rotting pants when over came a village elder clad in a loincloth and tattered red shirt. He beckoned us to his large round house where we ascended the primitively cut steps to be met by several families who all resided in the same shelter. Over their fire they were boiling plantains and rice for the evening meal. After we had hung our hammocks, I sat, tired, almost unaware of what was going on around me. The chatter of children and the routine of the round house seemed a long way off. John and Ian had the same vague, exhausted look. We were all hungry and wanting to rest.

"Why didn't the Rovers follow this trail?" Ian asked as he adjusted his position and continued to swab his leg.

"It was too awkward for them," John concluded. "They didn't go

▲▼▲

too far past Paya before taking to the water."

"Or maybe they took a short, straight try, then gave up to float to Yaviza," I joined in. Here we were, no Rover trail to the next village of Yapé and as yet no guide. We had nearly gotten lost because of the absence of a Rover trail, and it had certainly made the going much harder and slower. As far as we knew, the trail resumed at Pinogana, a small town seven miles from Yaviza. From here Pinogana seemed a long way off. We had naturally picked the shortest and most favorable route that had avoided river transportation. So far our overland record remained unblemished—we wished to keep it that way to the end.

I flipped the lid from the first-aid kit; there sitting beside the vials of adrenaline lay the final dose of Ian's penicillin. This last shot was a booster, a one-week supply in a single injection.

I knew Ian was tired and hungry, exhausted after the late afternoon run against time. Why not wait until morning? But Wilma had said to keep up the doses, every last one, until I'd finished. He saw me preparing the shot and suggested we wait until after dinner.

"Fine with me," I said, carefully laying the syringe back in the kit. His continual swabbing combined with the penicillin injections had taken effect; the redness was disappearing, and the punctured, festering holes were filling in and healing. At last the leg looked better. After dinner, before a crowd of interested spectators, I administered the final dose. His reaction was the same as usual. What could he expect from a man who had only vaccinated animals?

The next days were the same as those just past in the stinking, insect-ridden jungle. Local guides took us from place to place as we struggled behind them. Where was the fat rich gringo of the movies who carried nothing but a twelve-bore shotgun and a jungle safari hat? We had the guides, but there the similarity definitely ended!

On the twenty-fifth day from Sautatá (the second from Capetí), we broke clear of an old banana plantation to unexpectedly face a sharp drop into a convulsing river. The rains had been falling heavily for three days, saturating everything. The river was badly swollen. It surged, frothed, and boiled over rocks, carrying with it debris from higher up. Our packs weighed heavily on us, tugging at our tired backs. The thought of crossing it on foot chilled us. We knew instinctively that this raging torrent was far too strong. John climbed down the narrow path into water only calf deep and could hardly stand. It

▲▼▲

tore at his clothes and almost knocked him down before he was able to climb back out.

"It's too strong!" he yelled above the deafening roar.

"What is it?" Ian asked, just beyond earshot.

"It's too big. The thing's too dangerous!" I yelled back. I reached down to take John's hand and assist him up the bank.

"No way," he said. "We'll drown in that, ropes or no ropes!"

In the next few minutes God again demonstrated His mercy to three trail-weary men. As we contemplated our next move, a familiar sight rounded the river's bend. In the front of a large dugout canoe, straining against the flow, poled a young Chocó Indian. At the rear, steering as best she could, was his wife, and seated precariously beside her was their year-old infant.

We shouted and yelled to catch his attention, and he expertly maneuvered his heavy canoe alongside the knobby bank. Unthinkingly we piled our bikes, backpacks, and ourselves into that unstable dugout, setting the stage for a disaster.

We settled down low in the wet bottom of the boat, while the Chocó Indian pushed slowly on his pole. The turbulent water snapped the dugout one way, then the other way, then back again. The Indian strained to regain equilibrium without avail; we were swaying too violently. The sideway motion flung John into the raging water and I followed. Desperately we both reached for the submerged side of the canoe. Ian was half submerged and struggling to hold onto the three bikes. John was pinned back into the water by his pack. The Indian was holding onto the bow of the canoe, trying with all his might to right it. Standing in thigh-deep water, I snatched a bedroll and tossed it back into the canoe now swirling with rice, bananas, and water.

"The baby!" I cried out. "Where's the baby?" Horror filled my body and I was almost too frightened to glance behind me where she had been before we capsized. I looked back. There she was in the secure arms of her mother. Thank God!

We stood in the cold water, clinging for our lives, trying to right the dugout. Our bikes clanged and twisted together. We finally righted it and pushed ourselves back to the bank, not six feet away.

With white faces, we asked the Indian if he would make two trips across the river. He agreed and first poled across with Ian, his bike, and the three packs. They made it fine and carefully unloaded. The

▲▼▲

man knew his river, but foolishly had allowed us to overload his canoe. And the three of us should have known better, too. Just how stupid can a man become? Between us we had nearly caused the deaths of his wife and baby. This brought home to us how poor health and poor diet, plus the anxiety of keeping ahead of the monsoons, had affected our reasoning and ability to evaluate correctly. It could have cost us our lives.

In seven days we arrived at Yaviza on the Chucunaque River. We were only about halfway through the Darién Jungle, but we felt as though we had trekked a thousand miles. Mucus clung to our eyelids, sticking them together, exactly as had happened in the swamp. We became exhausted after very mild physical effort, sweating and tingling under muscular strain. At this main Darién town, we were to rest for three days. Tired and sick from days of jungle life and diet, we slumped onto the nearest bar stools and ordered the coldest drinks they had.

"Tres colas frias!"

Without hesitation the barkeeper placed the frothing bottles before me, but he checked the rumpled, wet dollar bill I handed him. "Viente centavos," he affirmed.

Ian, John, and our guide sat viewing our civilized surroundings. I gave each of them a bottle and then returned for my own. There wasn't one. I had forgotten about our guide. There were four of us. This time I ordered another five bottles. "That should make two each," I counted.

We guzzled the frothing liquid, thankful that, for now anyway, we were through with just straight water. We'd had enough of that in the form of rain.

On our thirtieth day from Sautatá, as we chopped a path through tangled undergrowth in search of the Rover trail, more rain fell. Sweating and blistering, we broke into a clearing to stand once again on a trail—a trail rapidly disappearing in rain and jungle growth—but still a trail. Now maybe we could push progress a little harder.

It continued to rain on us harder and more frequently, causing our boots to stick, slowing each of us, fraying tempers, and inciting thoughtless words.

Inside us lurked a feeling of desperation. Would we be stopped by another swollen river, or caught by another mire of mud? How much

136

▲▼▲

could we stand and still keep up the pace?

My stomach stirred, and I knew that I needed more pills but had none to take. Listlessness engulfed each of us and hung like a blanket, prohibiting any extra activity.

Ian's leg was now almost completely healed, but under the strain of being the least able of the three of us and trying and wanting to keep up, his effort fell off. John and I just could not carry more weight, as much as we would have liked to. Ian had to carry what we could not and try to remain ahead as much as possible. The danger of penicillin shock was past, so I quietly disposed of the emergency adrenaline.

When we reached Santa Fé, twelve days after leaving Yaviza, an infection in the inside of my left thigh which had been merely a lump at Yaviza had grown and was now a stabbing pain. I thought it was an embedded jungle thorn. I sat on an unpainted wooden stool in the warm tropical sun with heavy rain clouds looming on the horizon. The thorn burrowed still further.

"This is bad!" I exclaimed, drawing breath between my teeth. I relaxed, but the pain stabbed again. I flung my head back, hitting the wall I was sitting beside. My hands grabbed the swollen bump and held tight.

"Man, I've got to get that out!" I muttered under my breath. Sweat trickled down my back as I squeezed and pressured the growing infection. Many times on the trail when this had bothered me, I swore I would cut it open. Now, after experiencing the worst pain yet, I was determined to extract the thorn, but without the use of a knife, if possible.

Lips tight, I pressed until I could see the whitish end pop out through my punctured flesh.

OK, that's as far as you go! I thought, applying more pressure. My body stiffened in pain as I called for John.

"Wait a minute. Be right there!" he yelled from inside our roomy hut.

"Come on! I can't hold it much longer," I urged as sweat glistened across my chest and down my midriff.

"You know that thorn I had a while back? Well, I think if you grab the end there with your fingernails and I press hard, we'll extract it—if I'm lucky."

▲▼▲

Our eyes glued on the small protrusion encircled with blood and sweat, John carefully lowered his thumbnails.

A sudden stab of pain made me yelp, but I managed to retain my grip. John met my tear-filled eyes. "It moved," he said. "It's alive, Gary. That thing's alive!"

I swallowed, gritted my teeth, and pressed harder. "OK, John, let's get it out," I urged.

In a second a worm, almost three-fourths of an inch long and filled with my blood, lay on the stool beside me. Blood ran down to my knee. I turned away from that vile-looking creature that had lived on my flesh. I felt sick inside, but also relieved, as I dressed my open wound. I was revolted by the thought that I had been host to such a creature—the result of a fly laying its eggs in my flesh.

The wound had to be kept clean and the hole filled with antiseptic ointment to prevent further infection.

Our rest stop at the deserted logging camp of Santa Fé lasted three days. Then we left for the next spot on our map, the small village of Cañitas. It was on this stretch of trail that I would experience the most dramatic and revealing action of the hand of God. All that had gone before, although not insignificant, would be greatly overshadowed by this demonstration of His love. I was to come to grips with a situation for which there was no explanation, a situation that brought with it the wonderful understanding that God loved and cared for me, a twenty-three-year-old New Zealander in the Darién Jungle.

▲▼▲

13

God's Love

End of the Darién

Along heavily rutted logging tracks, we pushed toward the Bayano River valley. The Bayano, one of the main rivers in eastern Panama, would constitute one of the major engineering efforts in the construction of the Pan-American Highway. The logging tracks we followed sprawled in every direction known to man: crisscrossing, climbing, leveling, winding, turning, dipping, plunging. But at least we did have a track to follow, choosing with our small pocket compass the one headed in the direction of the town of Cañitas.

We spotted animal tracks we had not seen before, tracks that indicated the prowling area of the puma. His hunting grounds, as could be expected, were above the swampy, stagnant growth and in the towering jungle flora of the ridges and higher slopes. The prints of many cats appeared as we continued on. We could hear them growl and roar in the distance, and some came fearfully close. At night I now slung my hammock above waist height and wedged my sharpened machete in a branch just outside the zipper opening; nighttime squeals followed by rustling and other noise were common, so it seemed wise to keep the machete within arm's reach. Should I be molested by a cat or snake during the hours of darkness when the jungle came to life, I would at least have my best weapon with me.

For three months, since we had left the road at El Tigre, our goal had been to rejoin the road again at Cañitas. Now as we struggled along trails awash with stagnant pools, mosquito larvae, and slime, we were only one week away from our goal. Cañitas was only six miles on the other side of the Bayano River.

▲▼▲

The mire that had bogged us down for so long still stubbornly clung to our boots, legs, and bicycles. Under conditions that would have made progress difficult for a horse, we sweated and grunted. The logging trails had been softened by heavy rain and made worse by the movement of cattle. The signs of cattle encouraged us, for we reasoned that where they were, habitations could not be far away. Our exhausted minds tried desperately to figure out the distance, the time, and how much longer we'd be in here. Arguments between John and Ian had sprung up earlier in the jungle, disrupting their relationship; and now under the severe stress, tempers flared uncontrollably. I also had had all I could stand and joined in these conflicts. The lives we had led for three months, under stress and conditions a man was not normally called on to face, caused our emotions to rage unopposed and our ill-feelings to surge forth without check.

One day John and I broke clear of a patch of mud that had brought our pace to a slow crawl. We stopped to catch our breaths and watch Ian stagger on up a small hill in front of us. He strained for every inch and once on top slumped earthward, deathly white. He watched us as we, unwilling to proceed in his footsteps, looked for an easier way. John went up first; then I followed a little distance behind him, trying not to put my feet in the same places he had used. A grunt and a groan sounded from above me, and I looked up to see John clinging to the mud, his bike and body tangled, suspended, and about to plunge down on top of me.

"Hold it!" I yelled. "Hold it. Wait till I give you some bracing."

"Can't stay here much longer, Gary. My weight's on one foot and that's sliding away," he panted in reply.

With my left shoulder under his right thigh, we steadied one another. He untangled himself from his bike, took his left foot and placed it more directly underneath him, and pushed away from me. As he went upward I was propelled several feet back down the slippery clay face. Lying motionless on my belly, I followed John's progress as he showered debris and mud onto my face and hair.

"You all right, laddy?" John asked from above, smiling.

"Oh fine, real fine," I answered. " Just a bit further back down the track, that's all; but other than that, real fine."

My staggering reorganized ascent ended up being longer and more painful than either Ian's or John's. Amid a final flurry of leaves and mud, I sagged on the lip, face at ground level, gasping for what air I could find.

"Here, grab this," John said, offering his right hand. I reached up and together we dragged my aching body to its feet. I looked back. How slight the hill looked, and how difficult it had actually been to climb. Before this jungle trek, a hill like that would have only slowed us momentarily; now the effort to climb it drained us.

"Ian gone ahead?" I inquired.

"No. He's resting around the next corner. If he doesn't move ahead soon, I'm going to!" John replied angrily. He had readjusted his pack, cleaned the mud from his bicycle wheels, regained his second wind, and was ready to move.

In a few minutes Ian moved on. Every step he took was a nightmare for him. John and I were forced for the umpteenth time to wait almost twenty minutes to give Ian a chance to put distance between us. Impatience possessed us as we felt rain in the stifling, heavily moistened air. Rain would only slow us more, but it was becoming heavier with each passing day. Could we reach Cañitas in a week? This was the question that plagued my mind in these last days. It would be good to get out of here once and for all!

Striving for more distance, we precooked our rice as often as possible so each meal would take only the minimal amount of time. We used our Primus stove to boil tea, which took only a couple of minutes. The lunchtime break shortened more each day as we used every daylight hour for our struggle with the jungle.

Two and then three days passed and still there was no sign of the valley. Puma tracks continued with us, as did the distant howling. Just where were those cats, and how familiar were they with our scent? This was no wild thought. Big cats ranged in the area, and we could encounter them at any time. We were in their natural habitat, so what could we expect?

"What would I do if I found a puma in my bedroom?" I reasoned. "I'd kick him out in no uncertain terms! Well, I guess he'd do the—gulp! I hope not."

"Shh!" John hissed. "Shh! Puma!"

"Where?" I whispered back. "On the track?"

"On the right side. Over near that mud and coming over to the left."

141

▲▼▲

Ian was ahead of us, probably not more than five minutes' walk, most likely oblivious to our situation.

Struggling to lift each paw from the mud, and swaying from side to side, the puma crossed the track only twenty-five yards in front of us, tail looping with the effort to maintain his balance.

Neither John nor I moved a centimeter. We froze, eyes bulging, and mouth agape. The puma was either too well fed, too lazy, or too preoccupied with the muddy track to bother us or even offer a passing glance. Then he stopped, black eyes searching right and left in the jungle undergrowth, still uninterested in our presence, and with a quiet, streamlined movement he faded back into the tangled jungle just as quickly as he had appeared.

"Let's go!" John urged through clenched teeth. "Let's get out of here. Who knows how many members there are in his family!"

"I'm not stopping to count them!" I retorted, sheathing my machete and following John. Mud smeared our faces, shirts, and gear and flew from our heels and bicycle wheels as we sped past that section of track.

Ian turned out to be closer than the five minutes we had anticipated. The puma had timed his arrival on the track perfectly; he had passed nonchalantly between the three craziest things in his kingdom: one Englishman and two New Zealanders, all carrying bicycles.

Two more days dawned and died without encouraging signs of habitation or the Bayano River. The faces of my two companions were drawn and unhappy. I shared their gloom because, like them, my gut gnawed away inside, my head ached with fatigue, my legs longed for freedom from water, and my spirit desired rest.

In these intensely trying days of hope and disillusionment, my mind again and again went over how God had been providing for us. But as quickly as these thoughts came to mind, I threw them out, not wanting to acknowledge the help because I wanted to believe we had accomplished this entirely on our own. We had not had any so-called divine assistance, I told myself, only hard, gut-tearing sweat and blood. We had all suffered enormously, at times tearing at each other in vengeance for things said or done. Situations that had treated us kindly had been luck, nothing more. Who said any divine guidance was involved? I certainly didn't!

Although disappointed at not yet finding the river, I could look back and take pride in what we had accomplished in past months. We had struggled, suffered, and still survived—all on our own. The pride that rose up inside and made me want to pat myself on the back, also showed on my face. Inside was a feeling of accomplishment that no man on earth could take away or detract from. This overland journey from Cape Horn to where we presently were had made many different demands on my body and mind, yet I had faced each one and met it. Now in two days we would stand in the village of Cañitas—another triumph for me, another first, another experience nobody had ever had, another test to prove I was bigger than anything around. It felt good to know that I could make my way through the rugged Andes, scorched desert, and thick jungle and be able to say, "I did it"; to prove that I could fight against the land God put in front of me and beat it; to prove that by determination and dedicated physical and mental effort I could overcome. This is what I had come to do, and I had succeeded— God or no God! I didn't know that I was on the eve of being brought up short and forced to throw my entire life into His hands.

On the morning of June 23, 1972, the second to the last day in the tropical jungle, we rose early. It was wet and soggy. Breakfast was the usual oatmeal with white sugar. Nothing that morning suggested that after traveling 7,000 miles I was to have a personal encounter with God—a demonstration of His loving power.

Ian, as always, pulled out earlier to put as much time and distance between himself and us as possible. After washing our mess kits in a nearby pool, John and I packed to leave. We were tired, not yet fully awake, as we stumbled over leafy growth that grew along the logging track. Ian now had a good forty-five minutes on us, so we probably wouldn't see him for at least twenty minutes. Through a series of rest stops and water crossings, the morning progressed like any other.

By about 10:30 A.M., I became increasingly aware of a numbing pain in my lower left back. I concentrated on overcoming this nagging ache by ignoring it. This worked for a short while, but then, under searing jabs of pain, I finally faltered and stopped, leaning on the handlebars of my bike for support. Bending and then straightening my back, I ventured a few more strides to catch up with John who was just ahead of me. He glanced back but kept on moving forward, unaware of my pain. I covered a few short yards then called out for John to stop.

"Hang on, John," I urged. "My back's killing me.

143

For three months and four days the cyclists struggled through the Darien Jungle. Here, Ian, exhausted and unable to continue, rests on the jungle floor.

▲▼▲

He unstrapped the medical kit from his pack and sorted through an assortment of medications. I looked down at the supplies on the ground and then paced away in pain. I tried stooping, crouching, anything to give me relief. Nothing worked.

"Here's some deep-heat rub," he said.

"OK, rub it in and see if it does any good," I instructed, pulling up my wet, rotting shirt.

The heat of the ointment slowly penetrated the muscles. The heat felt good. I could now stand free of pain. For a short while at least, the discomfort was gone.

We repacked and moved on, thinking only of getting closer to Ian so we could watch as he crossed watercourses and climbed steep, slippery banks.

A second time I had to ask John to halt, almost weeping from the acute pain. John patiently removed his first-aid kit, really concerned now for my well-being.

"Really rub this lot in, John," I gasped, bent in convulsion. My hand filled my mouth, stifling a groan or scream. Something was terribly wrong. What it was I couldn't say; but if I didn't recover soon, progress for me was going to come to a dead end. Through mist-shrouded eyes, I glanced at my watch, 11:30 A.M. John must catch Ian, I thought.

"By the time you catch Ian, John, it'll be time for lunch. You'd better go ahead. I can't keep up any longer." This was the first time I had said those words on the entire journey, but now in the depths of suffering I urged him on ahead.

"You all right?" questioned John, looking at me with more concern than I'd ever seen from him.

"I'm OK," came my hoarse, choked reply, stifled by streaks of pain that now gripped my entire body. There was no use applying more of the medication, since it had no lasting effect.

Reluctantly John left me sitting on the track. He had taken my advice, probably against his better judgment, but I insisted that Ian might need assistance more than I. I was wrong.

With a rustle of leaves, John disappeared instantly from view through light, pressing undergrowth.

My aching arms reached for the pack. My legs were rubbery and weak. I pushed my bike forward along the path. A slight rise lay ahead and, with eyes nearly blinded, I saw first one, then two, then three sets of tracks. My pack dragged heavily, and each step took immense effort; my legs protested their ability to hold me up any longer.

Groaning and gasping for breath, sweating and shivering at the same time, I crawled to the top of that small rise, exhausted. Blinded by excruciating pain that engulfed my entire being, I released my bike and let it crash to the ground. I stood, trying to focus on the track, motionless, torn inside and out by racking fire that finally pulled me down in a confused heap to the ground. I lay entangled in the shoulder straps of my pack, moaning, gasping, and twisting in agony.

My entire being was in torture. I was alone on that jungle trail, urinating blood and vomiting, almost blinded by pain. I contorted and stretched, in search of some position to ease my suffering, but to no avail.

In those few minutes many thoughts flicked through my mind. Will I ever reach the road? It's only about six hours away. It might as well be six days! I'm helpless! Will I ever see my family again? I'm thousands of miles from home, sick and unable to move. You fool, what do you think you're trying to prove? What are you doing in the Darién, anyway? What do you want? What the devil are you looking for?"

My thoughts turned into fear, and my fear progressed toward desperation as I realized the seriousness of my situation.

Finally, I thought, Can God help me? Can He really help me now? There was no alternative my befuddled mind could invent.

My entire body ached from top to bottom. I lay twisted, broken, and beaten on the wet jungle trail.

"O God, I can't stand this pain or carry on any further!"

With a frantic effort, I crawled back to my pack, strapped it on, and staggered toward my fallen bicycle. Dirt and leaves clung to my wet body, excrement lay along the track, and the smell of putrid vomit rose in my nostrils as I stumbled from that place of agony.

Leaning heavily against my bike for support, I continued to fall and trip along the path. Yet, it was becoming clearer and clearer! "My eyes, they're getting better! There's John's footprint, and another." Soon my legs, instead of the bike, held me up. My chest loosened, and my breathing was no longer constricted. Then came a feeling of warmth, of well-being, of wonderful healing. My back warmed first,

▲▼▲

then my chest, and all at once my entire body felt clean with a health that had been absent just two minutes ago. My legs now strode out firmly. My eyes no longer saw double; they were focused and clear. The pain that had gripped me released its hold and I was able to breathe again and function normally.

God had responded to a sincere and utterly desperate cry to Him for help. He had given me what I needed. God had heard me! He was not dead. He wasn't a dream or a myth. He had heard and answered! He had answered me when I had no right to expect an answer since I didn't really believe!

"Thank You, thank You, thank You, God," I cried, saliva and tears dripping from my chin. "Thank You, thank You, thank You." Words of gratitude and appreciation flowed like a song from a man who was still dead in his sin, yet whose pain had wonderfully been removed from his body.

I cried for many minutes as I walked to where Ian and John were making lunch.

Ian met me two hundred yards from our lunch site.

"How are you feeling, Gary?" he asked, concerned.

"I'm OK now. It's OK," I choked, fighting back tears and trembling with the memory of what had taken place.

▲▼▲

14

A New Set of Values

Arrival in Panama

High above the massive Bayano River valley we stopped to scan the low-lying expanse of jungle. From our vantage point we searched for the river's edges, but didn't see a sign.

"Well, there's the valley," I sighed.

"Sure is," said Ian. "Now we only have to descend and cross; then it's a day's walk to Cañitas."

That news didn't elate us much because even a day's walk disenchanted our spirits. We were dead tired.

Nearer and nearer we tramped toward the river. The ground grew soft again, slowing us, as if to extract our last ounce of endurance. Boots were again sucked off feet, more mosquitoes plagued us, and our stomachs gnawed painfully. The roofs of several logging huts signaled the southern bank. With gasps and yells of "There it is!" we plodded closer and finally stood on the banks of the Bayano, a raging, swollen, mud-laden river tearing toward the Pacific.

We crossed the Bayano by dugout and walked along good logging trails into Cañitas. Now we had a firm track. Soon, tire marks appeared! The sound of machinery greeted our ears, and soon people passed us, not Indians but Panamanians working on construction jobs, clothed, civilized, friendly, and interested. Upon reaching town, we walked into a noisy bar and ordered something to drink. Cars passed us, slowing to gaze at three rusty-looking bikes and three sick-looking young men.

We stayed at Cañitas for five days of rest and readjustments; we reassembled our corroded chain rings and rusty chains and took a trial run before our ride into Panama City.

Our jungle ordeal from the El Tigre junction to the small Panamanian town of Cañitas had taken three months and four days. Trials and hardship had drained us both physically and mentally. Now we were a day and a half from the place that had seemed beyond reach during those desperate days in the Darién.

On Friday, July 1, at 11:15 A.M., we rode into the busy center of Panama City. Crazy motorists, battered buses, and fearless pedestrians crowded streets and sidewalks. The people looked bright and clean after the crudeness of the Cuna, Chocó, and other Indians. They smiled more readily and seemed happier, having far more than most South American countries we had visited. Avoiding pedestrians, we rode along the cluttered Avenida Central to our usual first stop in any city: the British Embassy.

We sat uncomfortably in the chairs in the gracious waiting area. Congratulations were flung at us from various sources; reporters smiled as they shook our hands. Under a barrage of questions, we told our unusual story, a story that banished smiles and turned faces serious as imaginations ran wild. Quietly and as explicitly as we knew how, we unfolded for them the events of our 300-mile struggle for survival. Notes and photos were taken, and our interview in the rushed atmosphere of the embassy lounge ended in a series of handshakes and an invitation to the ambassador's residence for dinner.

Our puffy eyes and grumbling intestines made the days uncomfortable. Friends directed us to the Panamanian hospital of Santo Tomas for a complete physical examination. Inside a week the results came back. Just as we had anticipated, every imaginable parasite from the Atrato and Darién had acquired a new home—us. The medical superintendent's descriptions were graphic, leaving no detail to the imagination. He explained that since the infestation was severe and had already lasted a long time, clearing our systems would be an arduous and prolonged process. After one week we were to return to him.

During the next week we dined on several occasions with the British ambassador and his charming wife and shared with them more of the dramatic details of our trip.

After the Panama papers printed our story, I received telegrams from my parents and brother. I had been so preoccupied that I had not written to New Zealand about our arrival in Panama. My family and

▲▼▲

friends had heard by nationwide broadcast that the New Zealand cycling team had successfully crossed the most treacherous part of their overland trip. These newscasts continued sporadically throughout that tremendous day. The phone at home in New Zealand practically rang off the wall.

My hands folded back the thick paper of the cablegram to read my parents' congratulations, pride, and thanksgiving for our safe arrival. A mother's thankfulness is not something a son can fully understand, but I understood enough, and I knew my father was relieved and proud, too. My own feelings were of strong love and a great yearning to be near them in this moment of triumph. Just the memory of their faces and voices brought emotions welling up that defied description.

I read the cablegrams from my parents and my brother again and again. A lump formed in my throat, tears flooded my eyes, and I turned away to hide the heartfelt tears of a man far away from his native land. I was the conqueror of the swamp, jungle, and the South American continent, but had been too concerned with my own problems and the congratulations of strangers to share my happiness with my loved ones. My heart shrank in shame. My rushed aerogram found its way home several days later—my first real communication with them in four months.

Congratulatory letters now poured in from family and friends, urging us to greater heights and to a successful conclusion in Alaska. They couldn't guess at the spiritual emptiness that filled me.

We had finally arrived in Panama, a major goal and our imagined halfway point. It signaled the end of South America, the end of a unique experience.

It was strange comfort to sit in chairs and relax in a bed again. We spent the first several nights familiarizing ourselves with hotel accommodations and discarding rotten gear. Ridding ourselves of hammocks, long trousers, boots, and smelly shirts, however, would have left us with a skeletal wardrobe if the equipment we had sent from Medellín four months previously hadn't arrived safely.

In cycling shoes and light trousers, we toured the city, taking pictures, seeing an occasional movie, and enjoying the cheapest Panamanian food.

We planned to stay a month in Panama and set our departure at August 1. Reorganizing our spare cycling parts, getting innoculations and visas, and buying clothing took a large portion of our time. Life settled into a simple routine once the initial flurry of our entry into the city was over. When the fuss of newspapers subsided, we settled into the quiet, easygoing existence of tourists.

Our accomplishments were important, it seemed, only to ourselves. So we had made the headlines and the newscasts. Now what? Other people had jobs and did not have sufficient time or interest to give us the VIP treatment. Our goals were important news for one day, but then life returned to normal. Now thoughts of the countless provisions of God and His healing of my body filled my mind. Our target of Circle City, Alaska, remained nearly 11,000 miles away.

During these weeks of preparation for our next stage to Mexico City we looked up our missionary friends from Paya. Memories of Paya village flashed into my mind as I shook Keith's and Wilma's hands. Glad to see us in Panama, they listened to tales of our trip from their tiny Cuna village to Cañitas. As he had done by the flickering lamp at Paya, here too, Keith ended our meeting by reading from God's Word.

Many questions came to my mind as I listened to him read from the Bible. But Ian did the asking and John followed, while I sat quietly listening to the conversation sway back and forth. The same strength I had observed at Paya was present in this room too. Together that July evening we talked about why Jesus Christ had been nailed to the cross 2,000 years before. We discussed God and creation. Many things went over my head because I was unable to understand such depth or absorb so much new information about Christ. To me the Bible was primarily a history book. Although I had studied the New Testament in Sunday school as a child, it had meant nothing in my daily life as I grew to manhood. I had thrust it back into obscurity and forgotten it, never reading it, only glancing at it for the brightly colored pictures and then replacing it. I was slow to grasp its message, but it nagged at me. Arguments filled my mind. Why believe? It's too deep. Just forget it. These thoughts loomed up again, exactly as they had in Paya, and blocked the message out. Once more the lure of a carefree life prevailed in my heart, and I felt no need for this Saviour. Why should anyone wish to save me? I was going to heaven! Being saved seemed ridiculous; from what did I need to be saved? It was hard to believe that God could have a bone to pick with me. I had not murdered,

▲▼▲

raped, stolen, or offended anybody. God knew that! In my own way I was remarkably close to the Creator. Hadn't He helped us to a tremendous degree in the jungle? Hadn't He actually healed me? Hadn't He personally made my exhausted frame well again?

Our stomachs satisfied that evening, we enjoyed the luxury of a civilized home as we continued to talk into the late hours. Both Keith and Wilma answered our questions honestly. Our questions and doubts and unbelief illustrated to them just how woefully ignorant we were of Christ's life.

A few days later the Lord led us back into the company of these missionaries. But He had allowed a certain amount of light to come into my life, a little more appreciation of what He had given me on that wet jungle track.

The Forsters' small daughter, Wendy, not yet two years old, smiled a welcome to us as we entered their house for a second dinner engagement. They were familiar voices in a strange land, wonderful friends who had different views on life. It was obvious that they believed in Jesus, but more than that, they loved us. Love had not been shown us in this way before. After another superb meal we lounged comfortably and talked about anything that crossed our minds. John had acquired a New Testament from the Salvation Army and had started reading the Book of Matthew, so he was full of questions, wanting answers. The spirit of love that encouraged him to bring up these questions was able to offer a believable answer for each. As in our previous conversations, the discussion centered on the Person whom the Bible called the Saviour of mankind, Jesus Christ. That night this Saviour came to be more than a story, more than a person from times past. He was a personal Saviour who was asking me to let Him into my life.

Keith was not a high-pressure evangelist, nor was Wilma. They knew their own experiences, stated what they knew to be true, and answered the questions of three bewildered men who were trying to understand the simple message of God's Son. We read about this message in letters of the apostle Paul and others in the Bible. It told about man's condition, his sin, and his separation from God. The same message also gave the remedy: His Son, Jesus Christ.

I started to evaluate what such statements meant to me. To my knowledge I hadn't sinned; the shortcomings in my life seemed

▲▼▲

infinitesimal alongside others around me. I was still adamant in my belief that I did not need to recognize my sin or acknowledge that Jesus had needed to die to save me. Through Keith and Wilma I was now aware of this supposed Saviour. I knew the Bible's stand on sin and how God had provided for my acceptance into His presence by the death of Christ. But I was not convinced that I was exceptionally malicious or foul. I selfishly clung to my long-held beliefs, to my ignorance and greed, and to my search for money, the good life, and material possessions.

The easier half of our trip was still ahead. Because it was somewhat more civilized country, the people there would appreciate our accomplishments more fully. We were sure to sell our stories for large sums of money and possibly gain other material assistance. For years I had nursed this determination to succeed. It had been fed by my own efforts and by observing ruthless men clambering and stepping on one another, hurting and tearing, reaching for the top spot, afraid of being trampled and forgotten. Striving for prestige and power like them, I was determined not to sink to the bottom of the heap, trodden down and punched out. Not while I had the strength to stand up and fight. Not while the world was at my feet.

I had independence. I could come and go as I pleased, travel here, travel there. "And God knows I'm not going to fall into gross, unpardonable sin, doesn't He?" It seemed ludicrous to give up such a life because some book said I was a sinner and could be pardoned through the blood of Jesus. "Now, come on!" I reasoned, "How can blood wash away my sin? Besides, I know I haven't got any sins bad enough to prohibit my entry into God's kingdom. It's still just Keith's trip. Really, if he and Wilma want to believe it, OK, but I'm still unsure of the whole thing."

That evening, as Keith drove us back to the hotel, we discussed other things in the darkness of the car.

"Bye, Keith, thanks for the dinner."

"Hey, you guys want to come to church Sunday morning?" Keith asked. "We could drop by for you at 9:30."

"Well—maybe. Well, OK," John said, waving, "9:30 then."

"Thanks, man. See you Sunday," I echoed, closing the car door.

"OK, look after yourselves," returned Keith. Shifting into first gear, he started his thirty-minute drive back to his wife and child.

▲▼▲

Questions still plagued me as we prepared for our night's rest. John sat opposite, engrossed in his Spanish-English New Testament. Ian flopped heavily on his bed, worn out and full. The discussion had affected him also. Each of us voiced his own opinion of things said that evening. Time drifted by as we lay talking. Just what would Sunday bring? None of us was enthusiastic about attending church. We had accepted Keith's offer purely out of politeness and appreciation for what he had done. We'd go to their church, we'd listen, and we'd leave. My mind closed down at last, and I surrendered to rest, my body storing reserves for the next leg of our journey through Central America to Mexico City. It was a pleasure to sleep in a bed and know that tomorrow held no struggle against mud, jungle, or insects.

Sunday morning found us waiting impatiently at the Santa Ana Plaza.

"How's time, Gary?" Ian questioned.

"Around 9:45. They should have been here fifteen minutes ago," I replied, watching the shoeshine boy as he polished my cycling shoes.

"There they are!" called John. "In that pickup!"

I hurriedly paid for the shine and clambered into the broad seat, now loaded with three extra passengers.

"How're things going?" asked Keith, as he circled the plaza to head back into the Canal Zone.

"Not bad. We've nearly completed preparations to get our bikes sprayed. They all need rubbing down and painting," stated Ian.

"When do you intend to leave?" questioned Wilma.

"August 1, we hope," I said in a definite tone of voice.

Cars crowded the parking lot at the Protestant church. I was nervous, not wanting us to be publicly introduced as the cyclists from Cape Horn. On the pathway leading up to the door, a sign proclaimed, "Curundu Protestant Church, Preaching Christ Crucified, Risen and Coming." The church was full and that set me thinking. Why were all these people here? Just what did they want on a Sunday morning in a church like this? The spirit of warmth, love, and friendliness generated inside these walls immediately convicted me of having set my heart against something they possessed. I sat awkwardly beside John and Ian, feeling out of place, not knowing where to look or what to do with my hands.

During the next hour and a half I listened to the preacher, joined in

155

the singing, and responded to the vibrant atmosphere. Again, in the short sermon, I heard sayings and parables that Christ spoke while He was on earth. It was precisely what Keith and Wilma had been sharing with us during the past weeks. Here it was again, plain and simple, with the ring of truth. Here, on a Sunday morning in late July 1972, I was being spoken to by the Almighty God who had healed me almost a month before. I sat riveted to my seat.

In the rack in front of me was a Bible. Soon we were asked to refer to different passages in it. What I heard made sense, and as I read the Bible, deep stirrings began in my heart. I'd been spiritually dead for twenty-three years but was awakening now to the truth clearly presented—awakening to the real meaning of life. I knew the basic message, but this man spoke with authority that came not from within himself, but from the Book we followed together, the Word of God. I had never before heard it outlined so clearly, nor had it been brought before my very eyes straight from the Bible. It was clear that I needed Jesus Christ as my personal Lord and Saviour.

That afternoon my mind kept returning to that thought. I couldn't even think about the recommencement of the cycling trip. I became increasingly aware of my need as the day wore on. That evening we returned to church for a song service. The large number of young people in the congregation surprised me. Many had attended the morning service, and here they were again, singing. Why? What did they see in a church service? And why did they attend in such large numbers?

I didn't know I was only four days away from becoming a member of their family, God's eternal family. I would be able to enter the very presence of the Almighty, because of my own acceptance of His Son, Jesus Christ.

During the next days John and I talked over what we had experienced, what we had heard on Sunday, and how we believed the message given. Seated opposite one another in the twilight of the Panamanian rainy season, we questioned our preparation for the Mexico stretch of our tour. All would be completed after a few loose ends had been taken care of.

Yet something about the trip now seemed false; everything it had meant was secondary to what now dwelt in my heart. I could detect in John the same longing for freedom, not from the cycling trip, but from an internal burden, one that only Christ could overcome. John talked about his folks and how turned off he was by them and by the hypocrisy he saw in some so-called Christians. Our feelings were identical, and we discovered in one another the same desire for a more solid meaning to life. In our tour of South America we had seen many things, experienced new cultures, faced a new world. Now we were becoming aware of our inadequate standing before God.

In those moments I found myself lacking. We both felt the need to believe the teachings of the Bible, but first we needed the comforting love and forgiveness of Christ. Any barrier that I had originally erected had been crushed by the overwhelming truth in the Bible, made easier to understand by a man of God. Through the witness of Keith and Wilma, the people of the church, the teenagers, and through the undeniable presence of God in the services, the Spirit of God impressed His love on me. He brought to my mind the memory of my helplessness in the jungle, the excruciating pain, my agonized cry for help, His answer, and my tears of praise. How could I be so unfeeling that I would deny a God whose love exceeded anything I could comprehend? How could I turn my back on a faithful God who had responded to my strangled, desperate cry even when I hadn't known Him? I knew that if I rode with Ian and John to Alaska, I would be shutting this experience behind me, following my own selfish, self-styled, pleasure-seeking existence. I could not do this. It had to be here. It had to be now. I had resisted the truth for twenty-three years, but now God had brought me before Him in a hushed silence and was asking me to accept His Son.

John and Ian left to walk around the plaza. I was alone. I read a small portion from John's New Testament and switched off the light. In the stuffy hotel room I considered my experiences and the feelings deep within me. I believed that God had answered my cry for help; I believed He had saved us from drowning; I believed He had provided medical treatment; most of all I believed He had taken care of the three of us during our entire three-month ordeal through jungle and swamp.

Yet, something was missing. Something still stood between God and me. I knew it was just what the Bible said: separating me from God and God from me was my own sin, clinging to me from the day I was born, making me unacceptable to God. The only way I could commune with my Creator was to open up my heart and let Him fully control my life. That evening, I knelt beside my bed for the first time in my life, empty and longing to be filled, searching and finally finding the answer.

My heart burst with emotion and my mouth confessed the sin in my life—the grudges, ill-feelings, and hatred, the self-will and pride. I cried, asking Jesus Christ the Son of God to cleanse me and abide in me, to save my soul and give me whatever He had for me. I wanted Him to take over, to sort out the hopeless mess inside me, to give me purpose and love for others, and above all, to help me live my life for His sake instead of my own.

I continued to pray for almost twenty minutes—confessing, crying, asking, and believing. I thanked Him for His great love and healing.

I arose cleansed, a believer in Jesus Christ who had died on the cross 2,000 years ago for the sins of Gary Bishop. Now He was my personal Lord and Saviour. And I knew what He wanted me to do.

▲▼▲

15

Shifting Gears

The shape of new life in Christ

From the day I turned my life over to Jesus, July 23, 1972, I seemed to thrive on a different plane, one high above the grubbiness of this world. It was no head trip, no charge of emotion nor desire to ignore circumstances. It was a soaring peace that only Jesus gives and only to those who search. By knowing Jesus Christ I knew what it meant to be set free.

Now I had a new purpose: to serve Jesus. I wanted to serve immediately and actively. Our cycling trip had not glorified God. It had been full of wonderful sights, beautiful cities, and blasphemous utterings; we had experienced things that many people have no opportunity to know, yet we still had not glorified Jesus Christ. Rather, we had tried to impress, holding up the trip to say, "Look what I've done. I am stronger, better traveled, and far more experienced than you!" Where was God in that attitude? Now I wanted nothing of it, so I turned to my Saviour for His direction.

If He wanted, I was prepared to abandon the trip, to stay and accept whatever He had to give me; I wanted to serve Him the best I knew how. The momentum of the now seemingly pointless 20,000-mile ride to Alaska ground to a halt. One of the hardest decisions of my life faced me: to go or to stay. It was up to the Lord.

If I were to stay, God would have to give me the means to support myself in Panama. I prayed and His answer stunned me: within the next few days the Salvation Army missionaries gave me work, more or less on a volunteer basis, but with a small income that would enable me to remain in Panama and work actively for Him.

159

▲▼▲

As time passed, I felt Christ was directing me to remain in Panama City. For what reason I was uncertain. He had given me insight into things that had been dark in my life for years, had given me love that I found hard to express, and had provided a bit of financial support. His direction to me was crystal clear. Now a fight began inside. How could I break the news to Ian and John? And how could I explain my new convictions about Christ? I would have to trust Him for what was to follow.

In the days after my conversion, I shared with John the meaning of my new relationship to Christ. He listened with interest and evaluated the implication of my new commitment to the future of our cycling expedition. I knew from our lengthy discussions that he was being turned toward God himself. What he said revealed his longing for meaning, and as he looked back at past events, he gave the credit for much of our protection and success to God. Now he also became a member of God's family. His new concern was to glorify Christ in his everyday living. So John and I were able to discuss together what we thought was the will of the Lord for each of us.

One thing seemed obvious: if we were not pleasing God, we could neither be happy nor filled with His Spirit. Even as I had become sure that the Lord wanted me in Panama, John grew more certain that the Lord wanted him to return to New Zealand. He needed to clear up relationships with his family, this time trusting in God's love, not in the weakness of his own human ability. We each came to the conclusion that we had to terminate our cycling ride.

We went together to talk to Ian. Late into the evening I tried to explain to him the reasons for my own conversion and its results. I mentioned God's provisions in the jungle; then I tried to explain what I felt was God's direction to me to remain in Panama and serve Him here. John also did the best he could to explain to Ian.

But Ian was not impressed; he rebuked us both. Ian and I had a bond created from experiences of the past couple of years in New Zealand and on the trip. Now it began to deteriorate. Our conversation grew stilted, then hot with mounting frustration. The opportunity to share had come, yet all I could do was infuriate my friend. He rejected what I said and finally, comprehending nothing, left to complete preparations for his departure from Panama.

Frustrated, I almost wept in disappointment. I had been unable to express fully the desire of my heart to Ian and had shattered his dream of cycling as a team to Circle City, Alaska. Christ had so clearly directed me in my decision to stay that I couldn't place Ian's happiness first, yet I felt I had not even halfway managed to present my case. Ian was upset and wanted to rid himself of us as quickly as possible. He seemed to feel nothing for Jesus Christ or for John and me. His trip to Alaska had turned into a god, one that excluded the saving grace of Christ. Everything opposed to the continuing ride, he cut out like a cancer, seeking only to further his aim.

Yet I didn't believe that anyone who became a Christian had to abandon all that he'd been doing before. I only wanted Ian to understand God's orders to me. And more important, I wanted him to sense the excellence of Christ and the help He offered.

For the first time in my Christian life, my relationship with Christ had turned a friend from me. The friendship Ian and I had enjoyed soured and grew cold. This coldness was new, a barrier I had not anticipated, but my commitment to Jesus Christ remained firm and full of love. I felt the comfort of my Lord. How could I forsake God, who had seen me through so much, in return for a relationship with one man who still rejected the Saviour I loved? If my relationship with Christ had become the issue of friendship, then I was aware that Christ was paramount and far more deserving.

This commitment to Christ would hold true even if the relationships with my immediate family were involved. During the months away from New Zealand, as we cycled toward Panama, my longing to be with them had become a powerful force in my life; but now love for Christ far exceeded even what I felt for my family. He was now the center of life. He knew my needs and anxieties, and only He could satisfy and give rest. He, not my parents, was the Giver of all things. My family could not give what I found in Jesus Christ. Yet, because of Christ, I wanted my relationships with others, especially my family, to be deeper than ever.

As it turned out, although my conversion and commitment to Christ came as a surpise to them, my family rejoiced with me, and a new dimension became apparent in our feelings toward one another.

As John and I continued to talk and pray about our futures, we found harmony in the Spirit, common love for Christ, and a friendship that flourished because, unlike Ian's, it was Christ-centered. We

▲▼▲

became very close. Good friends over miles of distance, across impossible terrain, and against fantastic odds, we were now more than friends—we were brothers in the Lord.

John's direction from the Lord was to return to New Zealand. How I wanted to see my folks and share with them the peace I had. Instead it was John who was going back, not I.

I shook his hand as he left the Tocumen Airport. Though we both possessed little more than nothing, we trusted God to give us what we needed. We promised to pray for each other. We already knew, all too well, that Jesus Christ looks after those who belong to Him.

The shining jet lifted clear of the shimmering tarmac, screamed skyward, and finally became a speck among the clouds. I had said farewell to the same physical man, but one with new life, new spirit, and new purpose.

The friends I had in Panama City and the Canal Zone I could almost number on one hand. My one true friend had just left, yet God let me know that He was near. I was not alone. John might have left, Ian might want nothing to do with me, but Christ's presence was stronger than any human's.

I found a place to live in a pension in a low income part of town. On my daily trips through the streets, through some of the worst slums and red-light areas, Christ came with me, caring, touching my spirit. "I'm here beside you . . . I love you . . . You are not alone." He comforted me with these assurances many times during the five months I lived there. With prostitutes and perversion everywhere, the friendship of Jesus Christ lit my life and overcame the severest temptations.

In my room I prayed, asking the Lord to show me what next. Impatience mounted as I waited for His answer. The weeks slipped by, and few prayers were answered. Still He spoke gently to me, "Wait, be patient, and trust in Me." I strained to move, eager to get on with what the Lord wanted me to do for Him.

Once when this impatience came to a head, I sat on my sagging bed and whispered, "Lord Jesus, I'm trying to hurry You into letting me know what You desire for me. Lord, I trust You. I want what You want, because You have all knowledge. Father in heaven, help my impatience, make me understand. Strengthen me because I'm weak."

As I opened my eyes, I felt a peace that only Christ is able to give.

▲▼▲

He was aware of all my needs. I would have to trust Him. "Lead me in thy truth, and teach me, for thou art the God of my salvation; for thee do I wait all the day" (Psalm 25:5 NAS).

Many times in the next five months impatience and exasperation crept back. Each time I had to hand them over to the Lord again. But each time Christ toughened my weak spirit with His eternal love.

I was compelled to tell others about freedom in Jesus Christ; newly-learned songs came to mind spontaneously. I learned that God's family had many members, and that Jesus was real to them, too. I met servicemen and teenagers who knew Jesus Christ, and we shared the things He was doing in our lives.

I saw people, my own age as well as older, pray earnestly week after week. I saw others, because of this prayer, enter the glory of God's family, forgiven because of what Jesus had done on the cross.

In a few months God gave me better living quarters. Ian, I learned through one of my many Christian brothers, had just left Panama City, riding alone toward Costa Rica. I hoped he had found God's will for his own life in his decision to finish the trip to Alaska and then return home to England (something he has since done).

For me, my life was full of Bible study, prayer, worship, and the opportunity to tell others about the Lord. The cycling trip faded away; the goals that had once seemed important were now insignificant. Christ was far superior to anything I could ever dream up on my own. "For to me to live is Christ, and to die is gain" (Phil. 1:21 NAS).

▲▼▲

16

Encouraged by God's People

Panama to Houston to North Carolina

The roar of the chainsaw was deafening as it ripped through the gnarled trunk of a tall jungle tree. Slowly the vines strained and snapped and leaves showered down from the heights. Then with a tremendous crack, the tree buckled as the wood inside severed. The impact on the jungle floor was immense as it crashed through the forest. For a few seconds the surrounding jungle was eerily silent. The ground around the jagged stump warmed to the new rays of sun. Saplings and undergrowth steamed. The heavy chainsaw rested beside us as we surveyed the next towering challenge.

I had returned to the Darién jungle, helping to make the airstrip approaches safer for Wycliffe pilots and missionaries. After becoming a Christian I sought opportunities to return to the same jungles we had walked through on our cycling trip. At this project at the Cuna Indian village of Paya we were to fell about a dozen tall trees. I had flown over these jungles on several flights and felt the nearness of tall trees on first and second approaches. From the air I often gazed down on miles of jungle stretching out below me and thanked God we had managed to walk through it alive. Flying was a much easier way of traveling.

Upon arriving in Paya, I was greeted by Keith Forster. He had a delightful surprise waiting. As we clamored out of the plane, Keith introduced a familiar-looking Cuna Indian to me. Estaneslado was the young Cuna guide who had taken Ian, John, and me along the jungle trails from Paya to Pucuro. Keith now introduced him as my Christian brother! Unknown to each of us, we had both accepted Christ as our Saviour since we last met. We embraced each other under the wing of

▲▲▲

the plane. Tears filled our eyes with the knowledge a spiritual rebirth had come to each of us. The last time we stood together in this village I had needed his jungle knowledge. Now we were both engaged in making an airstrip approach safer for pilots and missionaries. During the time I stayed in Paya, Estaneslado worked with me. It is an experience I treasure because it is a testimony to God's grace in two very different men. I took other trips with pilots and doctors to isolated villages to help as I could.

It was not long before other Americans in the Canal Zone learned I was living in downtown Panama. Soon the George Downs family, who were members of Crossroads Bible Church, insisted I come and stay with them. George Downs was working at the Tropic Test Center after transferring from San Antonio, Texas. My relationship with this family was pivotal to my Christian growth and economic welfare in the Canal Zone. Without the strategic help of this family, much of what developed in my life would not have been possible. God used them in many ways, from assisting in my Christian growth to vouching for my status in the Canal Zone. I shall always be grateful to them for their sacrificial love and their determined efforts to help me. Many times I must have frustrated them, but they were loving with God's great love. Their spiritual maturity was not easily offended or their love easily derailed. God was to mediate His grace in untold ways through them. I owe them something I can never repay, and because of their efforts, they share in my ministry today. They gave selflessly without any thought of personal gain.

Through my regular involvement in the College/Career group at Crossroads Bible Church my circle of friends widened. One evening while attending a church function I met Delores Creagle from Wichita Falls, Texas. She was in her last year of college and had taken a break to visit her sister and brother-in-law who were stationed in the Canal Zone on military duty. Little did we expect that from this first meeting, a deepening love for each other would develop. As our relationship grew we shared our histories, present circumstances, and future dreams. Then Delores returned to Texas to complete her degree, but we maintained our relationship long distance. We parted aware that if our love was authentic it could stand the test of time and distance. When semester breaks came we did our best to fly Delores to the Canal Zone. During the months apart, mail arrived every day in both mail-

▲▼▲

boxes! We were engaged in Wichita Falls, Texas, in 1973 and married in the Canal Zone on December 7, 1974. Again, it was the gracious help of Christians who made the difference. The Downs family and the fellowship at Crossroads Bible Church hosted and helped celebrate our wedding. The Lord enabled Delores' parents to come from Texas and my parents to join us from New Zealand. Others came from Colombia and Panama.

During those short years in the Canal Zone as newlyweds, Delores was church secretary at Crossroads. I was technically attached to the Overseas Christian Serviceman's Center volunteering my time helping in various activities. I was also studying gemology, intending to immigrate to America and start my own business in Houston, Texas. I continued my work in precious and semi-precious materials and secured a partnership in Houston, Texas, and we made plans for a new life in the United States.

My preparation to immigrate to the United States met some substantial delays. The delays were aggravated by my overland jungle entry into Panama. Entering through the "back door" was diplomatically difficult. The delays were further protracted by the proverbial bureaucratic red tape. I shall always by thankful to Phil Steers, then comptroller of the Canal Zone, for vouching for my character. After several unfruitful attempts to satisfy immigration criteria and being given the proverbial "run-around," Phil made one telephone call and my case went from "delay" to "fast forward." I had shared my situation at prayer meeting and Phil took it from there. Once again, through effective mediation of others, doors opened under the Lord's guidance.

Often we wondered how the Lord was going to break this immigration "logjam." Answers to prayers were significant markers in our journey as newlyweds. Not only were we praying as a couple, but others were praying for us. Delores and I often recall these years and remember the "lightning rod" answers that guided us then. Those experiences gave us strength that we draw on even today as examples of how and what the Lord can do. The Lord is doing those same kinds of things in our pilgrimage today.

Once in Houston, Texas, we established our first stateside home in an apartment and we went to work. We joined a Southern Baptist Church in Houston, and Delores began working in its daycare program. It was 1975 and Houston was a boomtown, so business for the

▲▼▲

partnership was growing. Underlying the business success, however, was a spiritual unease that seemed to grow from month to month. In mid 1976 we took a two week vacation to visit North Carolina and see the Downs family who had resettled there. They were active in First Baptist Church, Havelock, in eastern North Carolina.

The purpose of our visit was to renew our friendship with the Downs, but also to search our hearts for God's will. The unease had not diminished in our lives. Secular business no longer seemed the place where the Lord wanted us. This break was needed for personal reflection and prayer. While in Havelock, we met the pastor of First Baptist Church, Dr. Don Hadley, and his wife, Sara.

During our visit to Havelock we learned the church was considering adding a position for youth and outreach ministry. After much prayer and deliberations, a call to that position was extended to me. It came with a minimal salary and it meant Delores would need to seek work. Delores and I felt this was where the Lord wanted us, so we packed our belongings, sold my partnership in the gemology business, and moved to North Carolina.

The Lord continued to open doors as we settled into our new life in Havelock. It soon became clear we had not misread the Lord's leading. The call into the gospel ministry was right. From the beginning, the love and support of the members of First Baptist Church was a blessing. The fellowship opened their hearts to us and encouraged us at every turn. Encouragement from Don Hadley was critical to my growth and effectiveness at this time, especially since I was now attending college working toward a bachelor's degree. Don's encouragement to further my education was undaunting. In our regular meetings together, he encouraged me to focus on the big picture and long-term perspective of my life's ministry. He helped me see the various opportunities available in ministry and insisted I work towards this degree in order to meet entrance requirements to seminary. Don often made the point that anyone who could travel through South America as I had done could complete college and seminary degrees. It meant starting college level courses immediately, sustaining the financial burdens, and balancing youth ministry as well. It meant evening classes four nights a week and on Saturday mornings for 3 1/2 years and then straight into seminary for graduate studies.

"I'm pointing you toward a long, uphill climb, Gary," said Don.

▲▼▲

"But one which you will need to climb if you are going to reach your potential. I believe you are called into ministry and both you and Delores are capable of doing well. Get started now and the members of First Baptist Church will stand behind you both."

That advice was strategically important. I knew I was long on missions experience and short on academics. The next years would focus on long-term goals of earning my bachelor's and master's of divinity degrees. Delores and I believed it to be the way ahead, taking about 7 years of our lives to complete. We would trust the Lord to provide the funds and guide our personal stewardship of meager resources. East Carolina University offered extension courses nearby, and under the capable guidance of Dr. Bob Denny, we set our course.

During our time at First Baptist Church I was licensed to preach and later ordained to the gospel ministry. Ordination was a very significant event in my life. I wrote to my parents in New Zealand inviting them to make the journey over. Don Hadley wrote a personal invitation that tipped the balance for their flying halfway around the world. Others were able to come from other states, and the ceremony was meaningful to all. On October 2, 1977, I was formally ordained into full-time gospel ministry at First Baptist Church, Havelock, NC.

We managed a three week vacation with my parents before they returned to New Zealand. It had been their second trip out of New Zealand and would be their last as health concerns and age slowed their ability to travel such distances.

Saying goodbye is never easy. As Delores and I watched my parents depart for their flight, tears flowed. We didn't know what the next years held or when we might see them again. But we remained convinced that the Lord's way for us included finishing my education. Youth ministry schedules, study loads, and financial burdens pressed us. But encouragement from others is what we remember most, along with the underlying grace of God enabling us to meet the demands.

The opportunity to pastor my first church came in 1978 when Cape Carteret Baptist Church called me as their minister. Cape Carteret was a young congregation about 20 miles from Havelock. They were involved in a building program and they allowed me to continue my college work. I pastored, visited and preached, and went to college four nights a week and on Saturdays. Tremendous energy and balance was required, along with the ability to mentally change

▲▼▲

gears and be flexible. Delores deserves the utmost credit for tolerating many things during these years. I simply could not have done it without her gracious, loving understanding to our long-term goals in ministry. Our three years with Cape Carteret Baptist Church saw the completion of a fine new sanctuary, an education wing, and membership growth that almost tripled. The congregation was tremendous as the Lord grew us numerically and spiritually.

During our three years at Cape Carteret our sons Gary and Paul were born. We thanked the Lord for the safe and healthy arrival of Gary Keith on June 23, 1979, and Paul Douglas on July 10, 1981.

In 1981 I earned my bachelor's degree from East Carolina University, majoring in sociology and psychology. Stage one was complete. Stage two meant enrolling at Southeastern Baptist Theological Seminary at Wake Forest, NC, and leaving the Cape Carteret fellowship. Some members wished we could have stayed on and commuted during the week. But that arrangement would have been unfair to all, so we packed up and left to accept the call as student pastor of Rock Grove Baptist Church, Roxboro, NC.

Rock Grove was a rural church, well aware of its ministry to seminarians and their families. We lived in their parsonage and I commuted the 100 miles round trip on weekdays. We received far more than we ever gave to this fellowship. They were genuine people who loved the Lord dearly and knew how to accept us and share with us.

A new world opened up at seminary, as I finally studied topics directly related to my call. The professors and my seminary peers added much to my development as pastor. From 1982 to 1984 I functioned as seminary student, pastor, and husband and father. The demands were high. However, I was blessed with an understanding congregation and a loving, devoted wife. Time and again the Lord met our financial and emotional needs. Our lives were in His hands and although we had little in terms of worldly goods, we found direction, purpose, and grace for these demanding circumstances.

My first contact with a Southern Baptist Foreign Mission Board representative came while at Southeastern Seminary. During my second year I talked with Norman Burnes about serving with the Board. Delores and I felt God was calling us to return to foreign missions work.

As Norman and I talked two concerns surfaced. The first was the need to complete a seminary degree. We were on course for that. The second concern was my New Zealand citizenship. Persons appointed by the Foreign Mission Board must be American citizens. Since arriving in the United States I had had "Green Card" status, which identified me as an alien entitled to permanent residence. I had lived under this status for five years and knew the day was coming when I needed to consider my citizenship. Norman's words to consider changing my citizenship were not a surprise, but they needed careful thought.

Over time, Delores and I concluded that since she and our two sons were American citizens, it was best for me to become a naturalized American citizen. Our future as a family was in America and I had no plans to live permanently in New Zealand. On November 24, 1982, almost 12 years to the day I left New Zealand, I stood in District Court in Raleigh, North Carolina. With my right hand raised, I pledged allegiance to the flag and country of the United States of America.

I had sorted through the implications and decided it was time to fully identify with the country I had grown to love so deeply. I weighed the reactions of my family in New Zealand and reckoned they would eventually learn to live with my decision. To this day I think some family members are still uneasy about my decision, but I have no regrets and will press on to accomplish my ministry as the Lord leads.

In August 1988, I completed the last requirements for my master of divinity degree. Don Hadley had said it would be a long haul. Almost seven years from our initial meeting, I finished my preparation for full-time service. At last, at age 34, my missions experience and academic qualifications "joined hands."

▲▼▲

17

Vineyards and Perspectives

Appointment by the Foreign Mission Board

The sum total of my pastoral experience to this date had been in the Atlantic Baptist Association in North Carolina. We never expected to move back to the same association after seminary. We had planned to try to relocate nearer Delores' family in Texas. But the Lord had different plans for us. We realized the Lord had many vineyards of service, and our corner seemed to be in the Atlantic Baptist Association for the moment.

Following the usual referrals and interviews, we were contacted by River Bend Baptist Church in New Bern, NC. It was a new church in a new community, looking for their next pastor. River Bend was a mission of Temple Baptist, New Bern. In a conversation with one of the deacons, I voiced my concern about returning to the same association I had served in before. Most seminarians don't usually return to their "home" associations, but serve elsewhere upon graduation. The previous Director of Missions, Henry Privette, could see no problem with our serving at River Bend. Some of the members knew of my ministry in past years and welcomed us back as their new pastor and family.

The River Bend community was populated by a diverse cultural mix and was not the usual North Carolina composition. We were ministering to an upper-middle class professional community with many retirees from the northeast United States. It was enormously challenging to work with them those four years. The fellowship grew steadily from a core group of 44 and more than doubled in size. From 1984 to 1988 our ministry knew some of the highest joys and deepest sorrows. The fundamentals of church life changed and expanded as members supported the work with their resources and effort. My counselling load skyrocketed as people came into the community with little spiritual base or direction. Many hours were spent visiting people in expensive homes where spiritual interest was minimal and where the god of success was enshrined. There I heard some of the slickest reasons why people do not believe in Christ as their Saviour. From executives and managers I saw how difficult it was for them to come to a personal belief in Christ. I was reminded of what Jesus said in Luke 18: 24-25, "How hard it is for those who are wealthy to enter the kingdom of God! For it is easier for a camel to pass through the eye of a needle, than for a rich man to enter the kingdom of God" (NAS).

Alongside that were numbers of people who responded positively to the Gospel. They came by faith and followed in believer's baptism. Over time they involved themselves more fully in church life and grew in spiritual maturity. The church budget grew substantially year by year while other groups within the fellowship life broadened our collective outreach and influence in the immediate community.

During this time we began to appreciate why the Lord had brought us back to Atlantic Baptist Association. Over the years we had come to know and value many Christian friends there. In the past, I had led revivals and taken part in association life. In essence, we had returned to friends. The wider Christian community became the spiritual support base the Lord used to launch us back to the missions field. With Delores' parents in Texas and mine in New Zealand, we soon realized that our parental home base was diminished. Neither of us had come from a long line of Southern Baptists; both sides of the family strained to understand who Southern Baptists were. As far back as the early Canal Zone days, I knew my life and future ministry lay in the Lord's hands.

One day the phone rang while I was working in my office. "Hello, Gary. I just thought I'd call and touch base and see how you and Delores are doing. I wanted to ask if you have given any further thought to foreign mission work?" The voice on the phone belonged to Norman Burnes, Foreign Mission Board candidate consultant.

"At this time, we think the Lord is saying `stay put' for now. We are having a productive ministry with the people of River Bend," I replied. Norman had not forgotten our initial contact at Southeastern Seminary. He asked if I'd decided to change my citizenship. I shared

▲▼▲

how all of the Bishop family were now US citizens. He was delighted that our ministry was going well in New Bern and affirmed our work. Over the next few years Norman kept in touch with occasional phone calls.

What Norman didn't know, and I didn't share, was that Delores and I were beginning to pray about and discuss possible service in foreign missions. We examined our international perspectives and how we could best maximize our missions experience. As I meditated on these things and discussed them with Delores, it became increasingly obvious that my background had prepared me for service other than pastoral ministry in the US. Our years in North Carolina had been crucial to our pilgrimage. They had been years of growing and maturing, of educational opportunities and family growth. But the perspective we brought to our ministry was larger in scope than our present challenge. We had to seek ways of involvement in the missions fields of the world. We had been equipped with unique qualifications and perspectives. Although our ministry at River Bend was productive, there was no denying the Holy Spirit was calling us to a thorough re-examination of our future.

Our next steps were to seek confidential advice and prayer partners. Rev. Keith Hamilton was the newly called Director of Missions in the Atlantic Baptist Association, so I spoke quietly to him regarding our thoughts. Keith gave his full support to what we were exploring and covenanted to pray for us during the next months. I also spoke with Dr. George Shore of the North Carolina Baptist State Convention. Dr. Shore was a man of keen insight and understood what we were struggling with.

He understood our perspective and almost immediately saw the possibilities. His words were ones of encouragement, with insistence that I pursue this avenue. Once again, through the lives and minds of others, we experienced the Lord's gentle guidance to probe our future service regarding foreign missions.

In October 1987, I was invited to tour the Foreign Mission Board offices in Richmond, Virginia, with about 30 other pastors from North Carolina. We were briefed by various Department heads and shown Board home operations. It was a worthwhile trip that gave us an overview of operations and gave me much to think about. While at the Board, I spoke to Norman Burnes briefly. He was encouraged to see

▲▼▲

me there and promised to continue praying for the Bishop family.

In the next weeks Delores and I discussed in depth serving in foreign missions, its implications, and our family concerns. We finally decided to write to the FMB requesting information on options for service. A hefty package soon arrived along with a personal note from Norman indicating his willingness to answer any of our questions.

Delores was now working at the Neuse Mental Health Clinic, teaching mentally-handicapped children. One afternoon she shared with me that she had been offered the Director's position and needed to reply in a week. This promotion was a surprise and in financial terms meant a sizeable salary increase. Now we had to make a decision. If Delores accepted the promotion, it meant staying in River Bend and, for now, closing the door on mission service.

As far as we could see we had every reason to stay at River Bend. We were living in a new home in an excellent neighborhood and enjoying our church relationships. But we decided to press on as the Spirit led. If we couldn't give foreign missions our best shot, then we should drop it. It was time for a decision.

The Lord had put the pieces together; now we were called to take the next step. After studying the material mailed to us, we decided to seek career missionary appointment with the Foreign Mission Board of the Southern Baptist Convention. We resolved that if we were turned down by the Board for any reason, adequate explanation would be given. We knew all candidates undergo extensive screening before appointment and that satisfied us. We were willing to place our lives at the Lord's disposal, believing He had led in this reevaluation of our place of ministry.

By the end of November 1987, our applications were in process with the Board, Delores had declined her promotion, and we had enormous peace in our hearts. Letters went out to the Downs and Forster families in the Canal Zone requesting prayer on our behalf and updating them on progress.

Shortly thereafter, we were given several places of service to consider. They were on three different continents and represented priority requests from those missions. We had settled the question of serving in foreign missions, but where did we think we were called to serve? We were ready to go . . . but to where? Would it be Tanzania, Peru, Belgium, England, or France? All the Foreign Mission Board asked was

▲▼▲

that we spend time in prayer over these five priority requests. The prayer partnership by the Board was not pressure, but a sincere desire for us to discover which field the Lord was calling us to serve. It would be a crucial decision that would effect our family for years to come.

Over the next weeks as we prayed and talked, we felt impressed to explore the possibility of serving in England, and we requested more information. Initially England was not our first or second choice, but we were continually drawn back to reconsider it. The request was for a career missionary couple to pastor a small, struggling church on a large housing estate in Leeds, England. It represented a new partnership between the Baptist Union of Great Britain and the Foreign Mission Board.

With the additional information in hand, we decided to serve in Leeds, England, if we proved to be qualified applicants for career appointment. Once we notified Norman of our decision, several processes were set in motion. Now he could begin securing personal references on us and we could let the River Bend fellowship know of our intention to seek career missionary appointment with the Foreign Mission Board. When we shared our intentions with the church, many were surprised, while some were stunned. Others later confided that if they had to lose us as pastor and family, they would much rather it be to foreign missions than to another church.

The date for our candidate conference was set and our references began pouring into Norman's office. Our family medical screening was scheduled, along with psychological tests, personal interviews, family relationship evaluations, and financial evaluations. Our sons' educational histories and progress were scrutinized and evaluated. Their teachers were asked to provide assessments and references.

At every step our family was treated with respect and sensitivity by the FMB staff. Our view, that if found unqualified for appointment the reasons would be understood, still held. Nothing we saw through the appointment process used by the Board lessened this view. In fact, the appointment process left no stone unturned and continually reinforced its integrity as it unfolded. We were ready to accept FMB criteria for career appointment, and if we didn't match it, we could be satisfied the reasons were well founded.

As we reviewed the support package for missionaries, we realized we would need to adjust our way of living. I knew of others who were serving with different missions organizations and found life hard. The support systems at their disposal didn't match the provision given persons by Southern Baptists. Its comprehensive support is second to none and we count it a privilege to serve through the Foreign Mission Board. This continuing support is made possible by millions of faithful Southern Baptists across the United States who respond generously through the Cooperative Program and to the Lottie Moon Christmas Offering.

In January 1988, we were invited to participate in a candidate conference in Richmond. Here we met others from around the country who were preparing for mission service also. We underwent medical examinations, interviews, and meetings. The schedule was hectic as our time together was maximized. We met members of the staff who administer the work in Europe, shared how we had become Christians, and told how the Lord was now leading us into foreign missions. The Personnel Committee, along with candidate consultants, working with the interview content, test results, and references, would decide our suitability and potential effectiveness in England. In a few weeks we would know what that decision was.

One day not long after that the phone rang in my church study. It was Norman Burnes.

"Gary, I've called to tell you that the Board's Personnel Committee has unanimously approved the appointment of you and Delores as career representatives to England, serving in Leeds."

For a brief moment there was silence. Then I managed, "Norman, that's great news! We are delighted and will move ahead with our plans."

Norman continued, "The Committee reflected on the fact that there couldn't be a better matching of personnel to field request. Your upbringing in New Zealand and pastoral experience in North Carolina equip you well for the task ahead. Congratulations to you both!"

One of the next steps included a long-planned visit to New Zealand. The members of River Bend assisted us with the trip and paid my salary while we were gone. Loving and gracious, they understood what this trip meant to our family. My parents had not yet met our sons. This vacation would allow them time together before we left for England. At the time, Gary was nine years old and Paul was seven. Another important part of going to New Zealand was to share with

▲▼▲

my family the news in our lives firsthand. We had kept them informed by letter, but now we could speak face to face.

Nineteen eighty-eight was a year of immense change and travel. In February we visited New Zealand; in April we were appointed as career missionaries; in August we underwent missionary orientation. By September we had arrived in Leeds, England.

More than 13,000 people filled the Greensboro Coliseum on April 12, 1988, for the missionary appointment service. The ceremony was impressive, with Christian songs and powerful messages addressing missions themes. Delores and I stood together on stage alongside other colleagues who would serve in other countries. It was a moving experience just to stand there. Tears blurred our vision and the lumps in our throats strangled our singing. Keith Parks, president of the Foreign Mission Board, brought a message that challenged others to search for God's missions call in their lives.

Friends from the Atlantic Baptist Association attended, and it was a joy to share this occasion with them and to visit after the appointment service.

With our New Zealand trip and the appointment service behind us, we returned to River Bend. Our job now was to decide what to take to England. Most of our American furnishings would be oversized in our future home in England. Appliances and bulky furniture had to go. So we sold all our household furniture with the exception of my study desk, chair, and our wall hangings. Irreplaceable family treasures that we had gathered from around the world came with us also. Other things we gave away.

By the end of June most household matters had been settled. We decided to take the financial provision allowed by the FMB and refurnish a smaller home on the field. Some missionary families take their household furniture because reasonable replacement is not possible in their country of service. We knew from information sent to us by church members in England that we could purchase needed items there to make our house liveable. We hoped and prayed the funds would be sufficient! To this day we are glad we made this decision. It enabled us to purchase furniture in tune with our new culture and that fit household design. English houses, we learned, are not designed the same as American houses.

It seemed 1988 was also a year of saying goodbye. In June we said

▲▼▲

good-bye to members of River Bend Baptist Church. These people had been so gracious to us, supporting us and working alongside us. Other families and churches from across the association expressed their love and appreciation, too, and wished us well. In leaving the Atlantic Baptist Association we really were leaving home. It had been a spiritual home that had nurtured us from ordination through our first pastorate; from starting our family to completing seminary; and now it had helped launch us into mission service.

Atlantic Baptist Association has a special place in our hearts. The people there encourage us in our work today. Many pray for us and our work in England. A steady stream of correspondence flows between us as we work at staying in touch. We are particularly grateful to Rev. Keith Hamilton for his encouragement and assistance in several ways. The Association is filled with precious friends who are a treasure in God's Kingdom. They have often been God's instruments to shape us and our ministry over the years. They share our victories and challenges in England because they pray, write, and support the cause of world missions.

Before leaving for places of service, new missionaries spend several weeks in orientation and final preparation. The Missionary Learning Center (MLC) near Richmond, Virginia, was the site of our orientation. We arrived late one sultry summer afternoon, having flown in from Texas. We were pleasantly surprised to discover Norman Burnes was the new director of the MLC. We renewed our friendship with him during our seven weeks there, and on August 23, 1988, we said our final goodbyes to him. We had now known each other about five years. Norman had taken us from our first enquiries with the Board to the completion of orientation before leaving for England.

During our time at MLC we grew to appreciate the Center and those who assisted us. The weeks there were intense. We spent long hours in cross-cultural and mission studies, and we were expected to apply ourselves. The families undergoing orientation together became quite close. We studied, prayed, laughed, and cried together. We reflected on the fact that changes and challenges on the field would affect every family in our group differently. We would all return to the MLC after a first term, but most likely it would be at different dates.

Finally, it was time to leave for England. John Deal, then associate

▲▼▲

area director for Europe and North Africa met us at the Richmond airport for a final farewell. He visited with us as we waited for the boarding call. We appreciated his thoughtfulness and support in those last moments. Then when the call came, we shook hands and waved our last good-bye before beginning our long journey to Leeds, England. The partnership between the Foreign Mission Board, the Baptist Union of Great Britain, and the Yorkshire Baptist Association was about to become a reality.

▲▼▲

18

Forging a Partnership

Ministering in England

We were the last passengers waiting for our bags to roll off the luggage conveyer. Our five lockers and four suitcases were nowhere in sight. We were standing in Heathrow Airport, London, and had no idea where the sum total of our worldly goods were. Then we recalled the standard missionary "benediction" that we had often laughed about at orientation. It said, "May the Lord and your luggage go with you!" At this point we were sure the Lord was with us, but we weren't sure about our luggage!

We made our way to the claims desk, figuring our luggage was well on its way to Moscow, Paris, Berlin, or Rome by now. What a way to start our first term, and we still had another flight to Leeds! Just as we were completing forms, battered footlockers and baggage started rolling along the conveyer. A little worse for wear, but at least they were in the same country as we were. We gave a sigh of relief with the missionary "benediction" still ringing in our ears.

After clearing customs, we checked in to our flight to Leeds. The attendant greeted us with a smile and wished us well, although she was unsure how often we would see the sun in northeast England. We found our departure gate and collapsed into some chairs. Gary and Paul were almost dead on their little feet, and we were not far behind.

The wind made the small plane buck as we descended through thickening clouds of a dreary northeast England day. Rather than a smooth landing approach it felt as if we were going down a flight of stairs. We had left daytime temperatures of ninety plus in the States; below it looked cold, bleak, and wet. Maybe the airport attendant was right. Sheets of rain hit our plane as we landed in Leeds and we lost sight of the sun. Jetlag was now taking its toll. We were exhausted and our sons were past reason.

John Nicholson, Northeast Area General Superintendent of the Baptist Union of Great Britain, was the first to welcome us. "Welcome to England, Gary and Delores," was his hearty greeting. Once outside, we were warmly greeted by others who had waited for this day to arrive. Derek and Ruth Lunn from Middleton Park Baptist Church, Joe Wieland, pastor of Hunslet Tabernacle, and Harry Weatherly (from the Yorkshire Baptist Association) all welcomed us. Each had played key roles in arranging this new partnership. John Nicholson and the members of Middleton Park had discussed this partnership idea as far back as 1986. A formal request was later approved by the Baptist Union and forwarded to the Foreign Mission Board in Richmond. Then the search began for personnel to match the field request. Two years passed between the time the request was made and we responded. The church members sent pictures and information to us as soon as they heard of our willingness to come to England. They explored housing options, schools, and did other significant background work for us. We are indebted to them for their efforts and the labor of love it represented.

Keith Jones, General Secretary of the Yorkshire Baptist Association, also had a key role in preparations, working directly with the FMB's Europe Area Office staff in Switzerland.

Now we greeted these people with mutual warmth and Christian love. As the Lord had prepared us for England, so too had He prepared them to receive us.

We lunched that day at the Nicholsons' home, then went to the Lunns' home to stay our first week. Everything seemed strange to us. Fixtures in homes were different. Stores held different goods and were arranged differently from what we were used to. We were learning at every turn, from every conversation, every newspaper, and every store. We began learning from the time our feet hit the ground and we haven't stopped since. The biggest surprise was that we had to listen very closely as people spoke. Even though people spoke English, the Yorkshire dialect and terms were unfamiliar to us. The Lunns were most accommodating and patient with our endless questions as we struggled to get our feet on the ground.

Other Southern Baptist representatives to Scotland called to welcome us. The Turnage family, representatives to Scotland, traveled down to visit us. They oriented us as to how the United Kingdom Baptist Mission operated. (The organization of Southern Baptist representatives to a particular country or area is referred to as a mission.) We enjoyed their fellowship and appreciated their wisdom. As Foreign Mission Board representatives to England, we were directly related to other FMB representatives working in Scotland. Journeymen (short-term representatives) were also serving in Scotland and Wales. Slowly, we learned who they were and where they worked. Our first mission meeting in Scotland gave us opportunity to meet everyone and put faces and names together.

Our first family dwelling in England was a two-bedroom flat (apartment) above the local butcher's shop. We were fortunate to get that, as the housing market was going through the roof when we arrived. Church members arranged for its rental, repainted it, and redecorated it in preparation for us. We were grateful for their thoughtfulness. From this small flat, the Bishop family set about understanding the local neighborhood and people, banking procedures, grocery shopping, and schools. We became acquainted with community leaders and citizens and made plenty of mistakes. But we learned, and we are still learning.

Our arrival was timed to give Gary and Paul a few weeks to adjust before starting school. We met their headmasters, visited their classrooms, and expressed our keen parental interest in their academic progress. We had been involved parents in North Carolina, keeping up with their academic progress. Now that we all faced new challenges, our concern for them was paramount.

Initially, the peer pressure at school was harsh. Both of them had good days and bad days, but through the challenges the Lord kept His hand on them. Many days they sustained verbal abuse and were reduced to tears simply because they were different. Other days, they were put on pedestals because they had come from America. In each experience we hurt with them, as every parent does, and witnessed God's grace strengthen them. We admired their courage and character as they learned how to survive at school. Both are now young believers in Christ, learning how to live out their faith in England.

Delores volunteered at their schools, which gave her an inside look at the school system. We wanted to make a positive contribution toward the schooling of our sons. This contact proved productive and

▲▼▲

enabled us to explain to people who we were and what we were doing in England. It also helped us understand the community and cultural expectations. We learned a great deal from her involvement. Delores' experience and training gave her good insight and keen perception. Our prevailing interest conveyed our love and concern to the boys. This was a key motivation for them to do well. Academic achievements were celebrated as a family at their favorite restaurants.

We spent the month of September shopping for household furniture and appliances. Making our American dollars stretch to achieve value for British pounds was a real challenge. Still, through careful stewardship and choices, we managed. We also viewed houses for sale in the area, and after a long search found a home the Foreign Mission Board purchased for our use in Middleton.

My formal induction as pastor of Middleton Park Baptist Church occurred on October 2, 1988. Baptist leaders from around the area attended, with the United Kingdom Baptist Mission represented by the Turnages from Scotland.

By November 1988, we had moved from our flat above the butcher's shop to our permanent home not far away. It was a small three bedroom house of about 1100 square feet. Now we went about the task of making it a home. As new furniture arrived and familiar wall hangings went up, it began feeling like one.

The Lord had sent us to an area teeming with needy people. Middleton Park Baptist Church is a small congregation located on a housing estate of about 8,000 people. It was the only evangelical witness to the people and was struggling for its life. Our ministry was to lead the church, stabilizing and strengthening it. Recent renovations to the church interior had done much to invigorate this small fellowship of about 20 members. It had experienced a difficult past, but members were confident a new day was dawning. Our aim is to serve the people of Middleton Park in the spirit of Christ. Our intended term is between three and five years, then transferring to another ministry position in England. Before our arrival, Joe Wieland served as interim pastor at Middleton Park while also pastoring Hunslet Tabernacle. Joe had a good ministry for two years and led the people in unity and love. We built upon that foundation, bringing our unique gifts and talents to the ministry. We started where the people were. We visited them, hosted them in our home, and joined them in various activities as we tried to

▲▼▲

understand the dynamics of their world.

There are thousands of estates like Middleton Park in the United Kindgom. Living on estates is very different from life in North Carolina, USA. Many areas are economically deprived, rundown, and buffeted by neglect. The social dynamics are different and family life is often harsh. Many families do not own their home or car. Children often lose interest in school and drop out at an early age. They enter an increasingly technical job market underskilled and with little hope of advancement. Personal and family contact with the church does not occur in great numbers. Children participate in church life, but often peer pressure will take them away when they are 13 or 14 years old.

In communities like this, personal faith in Christ as Saviour is not common. Nevertheless, we have found that the Lord has His people everywhere, including Middleton Park estate. Church members here are more committed than many church members in American churches. Approaches to evangelism, discipleship, and financial stewardship are very different. Our ministry to the people has yielded fruit because we were prepared to listen first. Our credibility has been earned by faithful and consistent ministry and witness. A big mistake would have been to come into this community armed with "programs" from another culture and expect them to work. Even with our readiness to listen and consult, we still made mistakes. Our minds wanted to race ahead of both people and opportunities. One of the results of our approach, however, has been the growth and strengthening of Middleton Park Baptist Church, just what we came to achieve.

One of the Scriptures that forms the basis for our ministry here is 1 Corinthians 2:1-5:

> When I came to you, brethren, I did not come proclaiming to you the testimony of God in lofty words or wisdom. For I decided to know nothing among you except Jesus Christ and him crucified. And I was with you in weakness and in much fear and trembling; and my speech and my message were not in plausible words of wisdom, but in demonstration of the Spirit and power, that your faith might not rest in the wisdom of men but in the power of God (RSV).

These verses sum up the hopes and aims of our ministry in Leeds. The

▲▼▲

Lord is building this fellowship again. We are working with church members, trying to bring new ministry, new confidence, and new witness to it. We realize Christ must be central to this renewed effort and He must empower our walk. Our involvement is fruitful as the church strengthens and grows by the power of the living God.

The familiar patterns of church life in Southern Baptist churches are not found in England. The fully-developed church program sought by so many American families is scarce in the United Kingdom. Church is done differently. There are different worship patterns, different music, and different leadership expectations. England is a different culture from America. But the focus on Jesus Christ as Saviour and Lord is the same. We share fellowship with fine Christian people. We sense our oneness in Christ, a kindred spirit in the Gospel and an abiding sense of brotherhood that transcends cultural boundaries. The family of God is multinational and multiracial. Our privilege is to participate with English Baptist leaders and friends in the new things the Spirit of God is doing in England. As we work within this new partnership with the Baptist Union of Great Britain and the Foreign Mission Board, we hope it will be an expanding reality to the glory of God.

I often reflect on the journey through South America–for what it held and the hopes interwoven in its unfolding. The challenge gripped my heart and life. The sheer physical and emotional stamina required drew me toward this enormous journey from the bottom of the world to the top.

But this was not only a physical journey. It became a deep spiritual journey, also. God worked through people and events to bring the dawning of new dimensions into my life that would last into eternity.

Goals that were previously focused on places and things became blurred as the spiritual journey gathered in urgency, reality, and power. Following Christ is the most absorbing, fulfilling challenge I could ever face. As the years pass, the Lord continues to build many new things into my life.

My overseas experiences are filtered through a distinctly Christian lens. I often reflect on the way God has led and blessed. Who would have imagined that I would marry a wonderful girl from Texas and then feel called into Christian ministry? Year upon year, Delores and I see God dealing with us. We have learned to appreciate what He has

▲▼▲

built into our ministry, enriching and challenging us. Because we were faithful with what He placed in our lives, we were led still further. At any point we could have said no and stayed where we were. At those important crossroads, we felt led to say yes to what we knew was God's call. When we moved in faith, the Lord opened doors of opportunity beyond our praying. Everything seemed to build upon what had preceeded in our lives. Now, through the Holy Spirit's leadership, we are touching lives in places we never dreamed. Delores and I often look at each other in sheer amazement at what the Lord is doing with us. We have a strange sense of becoming. As we take inventory, we see all that we have become is being used in ministry to others today. It is both an exhilirating and humbling thought.

I have often been asked if I would go through the jungle experience again. My answer is no, but if that is the only way a person can be reached for Christ, then yes. I am aware of how patiently God brought me to the point of knowing my need. It was a spiritual journey wrapped up in enormous physical challenge few experience. One of my favorite hymns is "Amazing Grace," for it vividly captures some of my experiences. I often wonder where I'd be today if it were not for God's grace in Christ to me. Almost 20 years into my Christian pilgrimage, the people and places surrounding my conversion are still filled with deep emotion. Coming to Christ dramatically changed my life.

At the beginning of our cycling trip I was lured by the carefree life and the hope of fame and money. The journey was high adventure, and I'll never regret it.

But the good had to make way for the best. Christ showed me how empty my life was, and He filled it. He showed me how poor I was, and He enriched me. He showed me that my indifference to Him was the heart of my weakness, and He gave me the gift of faith in Him.

My journey northward became a journey upward. But my experience isn't unique. He wants to do the same for everyone. Anyone who confesses his sin and trusts in Christ will find what I found: forgiveness and new life.

In these last years of the twentieth century, the Gospel will gather new impetus as Christians around the world share the Good News. With the fall of eastern European Communism and the changes to the European Common Market in 1992, the call for our commitment to

▲▼▲

missions has never been greater. Can we do what the Lord is asking? Will we? We have the technology, funding, know-how, and potential. The vineyards of the world cry out for the refreshing waters of Life. The Lord uses people, people like us, people like you. Gifted and talented, equipped and made ready, He then sends us into the ripening harvests of the world.

> And Jesus went about all the cities and villages, teaching in their synagogues and preaching the gospel of the kingdom, and healing every disease and every infirmity. When he saw the crowds, he had compassion for them, because they were harassed and helpless, like sheep without a shepherd. Then he said to his disciples, 'The harvest is plentiful, but the laborers are few; pray therefore the Lord of the harvest to send out laborers into his harvest' (Matt. 9:35-38, RSV)